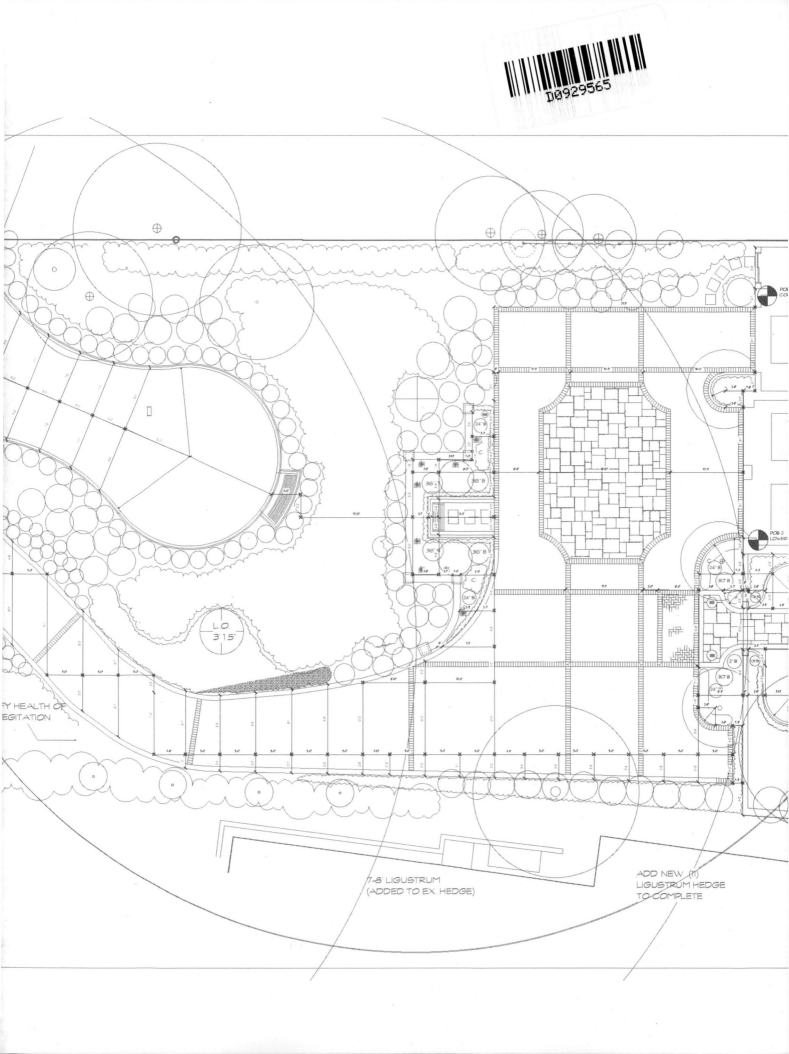

...FY HEALTH OF
...EGITATION

7-8' LIGUSTRUM
(ADDED TO EX. HEDGE)

ADD NEW (11)
LIGUSTRUM HEDGE
TO COMPLETE

POB 2
LOWER

LO
3'15'

Timeless Landscape Design

Timeless Landscape Design

THE FOUR-PART MASTER PLAN

MARY PALMER DARGAN, ASLA
HUGH GRAHAM DARGAN, ASLA

712
DAR

Wyrick & Company

AN IMPRINT OF GIBBS SMITH, PUBLISHER

Salt Lake City | Charleston | Santa Fe | Santa Barbara

First Edition

11 10 09 08 07   5 4 3 2 1

Published by Wyrick & Company
An imprint of Gibbs Smith, Publisher
P.O. Box 667
Layton, Utah 84041
Orders: 1.800.835.4993
www.gibbs-smith.com

Designed by Deibra McQuiston
Printed and bound in Hong Kong

Library of Congress Control Number: 2006927987
ISBN 13: 978-0-941711-85-2
ISBN 10: 0-941711-85-4

Contents

Acknowledgments

Hugh and I currently enjoy careers that jointly span more than sixty-five years. So, it is with great appreciation that we thank our mentors in design education. Be they educators or orators, brick masons or carpenters, landscape contractors, horticulturalists or nurserymen, their gentle gifts of inspiration flowed from books and the classroom into the field where all great ideas are tested.

How did we become designers? Hugh thanks his grandmother, who helped him make a garden at the age of four. As an Eagle Scout in Darlington, South Carolina, he learned to honor the outdoors and to set goals for his life. His great-aunts shared their love of garden plants and propagation techniques of hostas, ligularias and camellias. We grew up in different parts of the South and each had large lawns used for birthday parties, weddings and competitions. In my great-grandmother's garden rooms in Nashville's Belle Meade, pink-trumpet daffodils bloomed in the spring. Dykes Medal-winning bearded irises hybridized by Jesse Wills, a close neighbor, fugitive poet and dearly loved cousin, were wedding gifts to my mother.

Parents give in unexpected ways. Father, who loved to travel, fully experienced cultures. On our little Indian walks with the Girl Scouts, he would interconnect a bird call with an image in a great European painting or a sound in a musical piece. Mother, a retired businesswoman after three decades, loves historic house museums and works of art and excels in extending hospitality. They graciously allowed me to explore the world and to seek my purpose.

Our editor, Pete Wyrick, who helped us nurture this book for twenty years, believed it would finally happen. By sifting through the mass of information, he crystallized pearls of knowledge and helped bring atmospheric photographs into focus. He is a patient saint. Our publisher, Gibbs Smith, went out on a limb to support the authors' quest to communicate design principles. We are most grateful for this rare opportunity.

Kate Bennett, our dear friend and early editor, took our lectures and made them into poetic paragraphs. We are endlessly thankful for her work in the early stages of this book.

No designer can create hundreds of built works without visionary clients. It is true that you are only as good as the commissions you receive. We thank them for their patience during construction and friendship at the garden christenings. Our devoted team of support staff, including interns from around the world, enabled us to produce works on paper that communicate the design intent and the implementation secrets that ultimately make us look good. We especially thank Eddie Browder, ASLA, who, during a decade, made the transition from Charleston to Atlanta with us and ultimately from the drafting table to the digital world.

My landscape architecture students at Clemson University and adult students in the Certificate of Landscape Design Course enthusiastically encouraged us to write this book in order to explain our residential design process to others. The teaching of this material continues to be a rich experience.

Many thanks go to the friendship of professional photographers, including Maia Highsmith of Special Gardens, Pauleetta Atwood, and particularly Alexander L. Wallace, who took the time to teach us the art of photography so we could capture these ephemeral gardens when opportunity knocked. Recently, making the film transition from 35mm and Hasselblad medium format to digital medium has been an image management experience for me that, in itself, is the best teacher. More than 7,000 images were sifted through to glean the final choices for this book. You have to stop somewhere. A designer is always in love with current projects, which need to mature further and are necessarily left for future books.

Landscape and architectural historic preservation groups, especially The National Trust in England and the Garden Conservancy in America, are to be thanked for perpetuating the visions of owners and designers. By introducing the public to experience exemplary built works of art, high standard of future designs are encouraged.

Botanical gardens such as Cheekwood in Nashville, Tennessee, and Brookgreen Gardens in South Carolina played a large role in our formative years of studying plants and their habitats. We heartily acknowledge environmentalists who recognize the *genius loci,* or spirit of a place, and work diligently to conserve its natural beauty.

We thank the English-Speaking Union of America, which provided the grant to study the evolution of Jan Kip's eighteenth-century landscape drawings in Gloucestershire and to the Earl of Wemyss and his son, Lord Neidpath, who opened the doors of Stanway to our research. As a result, we've been canvassing England to uncover garden secrets ever since. The National Trust enabled our research at Newark Park, where we met the late Bob Parsons, who filled the sixteenth-century Tudor hunting box and landscape with life.

English garden writers, particularly those for *Country Life*, include Sir Roy Strong and the late Julia Trevethan Oman, the late Rosemary Verey, Penelope Hobhouse, Beth Chatto, Anita Periere, Mary Keen, and the late Sir Christopher Lloyd either befriended us, published our designs or accompanied us on visits to their gardens. Their written and built works provided inspiration to push the envelope of our designs with regard to plant material choices that consider each garden to

be a nursery of delights. Gillian and Paul Sladen, our friends in Bath, hosted us with many an alfresco picnic under their catalpa tree vista and adventured with us to gardens in haute Normandy. We thank them for introducing us to Sir Harold Peto's work at Iford and Buscot.

To all the British, American, French, Italian and Portuguese gardeners and garden historians who share the passion for garden design, we offer our endless thanks for your inspirations and ability to keep these treasures alive.

In the U.S., the Historic Charleston Foundation and the Preservation Society of Charleston keep the city treasures protected despite pressures of the times. To the families of the late Emily Whaley and Juliette Staats, we so appreciated your friendship and encouragement to the (then) young landscape architect couple who passionately wanted to understand Charleston's garden rooms, especially those designed by Loutrell Briggs. Dargan Landscape Architects' works on paper are now housed in the archives of the South Carolina Historical Society in Charleston and the Cherokee Garden Library in Atlanta, and we are honored by their ongoing preservation.

The Garden Club of America is acknowledged for its work in archiving garden design, education in horticulture and conservation programs. The American Society of Landscape Architects and the Association of Professional Landscape Designers present awards for outstanding designs and publish residential works to encourage others to excel in this art

form. We especially thank the ASLA for our national and state awards early in our careers, for these propelled our talents to larger audiences.

To the Garden Writers Association of American, garden writers, authors of books, shelter magazines and television media, especially HGTV's *Ground Breakers*, we thank you for your programs and for requesting the use of our photography and quotes in more than 300 publications to date. We enjoy the collaboration and hope the images are inspirational to designers and homeowners.

Rosemary Verey's tireless dedication as a lecturer, writer, and teacher spurred us on to write this book. She encouraged our efforts and has been a continual inspiration. The last letter we received from her before she passed away ended with the postscript, "Of course I'll write you a foreword." We feel she is in this book in spirit, and we hope she likes it.

Lastly, to my fantastic husband, Hugh Graham Dargan, ASLA, without whom this design conversation would not have started, thank you for sharing your tireless ear and keen eye.

—Mary Palmer Dargan, ASLA, APLD, CLARB, RLA

Foreword

The art of garden making is as old as mankind, and while size, style, materials and details have changed, the design process responsible for creating great gardens has remained the same. Building on the time-tested lessons derived from both European and American gardens, landscape architects Hugh and Mary Palmer Dargan have fashioned a personalized approach to garden design that has proven invaluable in the design of literally hundreds of notable and award-winning gardens.

Now in this newly published book, this highly talented husband and wife team share the secrets of their success through an insightful approach to garden design, developed and refined from more than thirty-five years of experience in residential design. Relying on the basic design principles of proportion, balance, harmony, rhythm and scale—complemented by a keen understanding of the genius of place—the authors offer a four-step master planning process that can be easily understood and applied to sites ranging in size from a courtyard space to a country estate.

In addition to explaining the application of the four-step master planning process, Hugh and Mary Palmer provide a personal selection of historic and contemporary gardens as a means of educating and inspiring the reader as to potential styles, materials and construction details. Additionally, a variety of garden features including terraces, pools, patios, arbors, gates and steps are included as a means of enhancing and enriching any garden space.

The ideas offered in this exciting new book will benefit and appeal not only to the average homeowner but to everyone interested in heightening their design skills. Unlike other publications on garden design, which focus almost exclusively on visual images to convey their message, this comprehensive work is unique in that it provides, in a logical and readable manner, a step-by-step process that is the culmination of years of experience in designing some of today's most creative and imaginative gardens.

—James R. Cothran, FASLA
Landscape Architect and Garden
Historian

This classically designed pavilion in Charlotte, North Carolina, is on an axis with the living room window and offers a captured view to the pool terrace.

Ars Longa, Vita Brevis–
"Art Lives Forever, Life is Short."

Introduction

Timeless Landscape Design: The Four-Part Master Plan reflects a thought process that is much more than garden design. It's a way of looking at a property as a whole, visualizing relationships between a house and its grounds, and ultimately understanding how to bring out a property's full potential in the most stylish, sophisticated and original way possible. It reflects how we think as professional landscape architects and what we actually do for our clients.

We have spent the past thirty-five years of our lives designing residential landscapes. It took many years of travel to study time-honored practices in Europe and America, and working on hundreds of projects to gradually formulate our own design philosophy and procedures. While techniques for analyzing a property and drawing up a master plan are now second nature to us, we realize this process is somewhat mysterious to most non-professionals. This book offers a vocabulary for designing residential landscapes that makes the planning process more vivid, accessible and easy to talk about.

Homeowners, educators, designers of all fields, architects, engineers and garden center staff will benefit from the emphasis on the domestic projects in this book.

Can you "see the forest for the trees" on your property? How do you unleash the potential of your landscape to touch, move and inspire your daily life? A master plan is the key to a timeless, fully functional property. This universal organizational concept consists of four interconnected parts: the approach and arrival sequence, the hub, the perimeter and passages to destinations.

A master plan consisting of four parts is inherent in every property, of any style, regardless of size. If your property is a townhouse, mountain retreat or large estate, the design process outlined in this book will enable you to fully express your grounds by offering a wealth of design ideas, material suggestions, planting design techniques and problem-solving tricks. The four parts of the master plan guide selection of plant materials, hardscapes and landscape structures used to shape and accent spaces. Shortcuts are included to assist in choosing sizes, shapes, colors and amounts of materials. Construction details, checklists and samples of materials make designing a fully functional home landscape a breeze.

The book is divided into five sections. The first describes the art, design process and historical considerations that designers use to execute their craft. The other four sections describe the internal workings of the four key parts to the master plan. Anatomical descriptions of each part are intended to aid in the visualization of your future landscape. A lexicon, or language of the land, is included after each chapter to reinforce design concepts.

Now relax; it is time to take your property to school!

part one

Sources and Inspiration

ART, DESIGN PRINCIPLES AND THE HISTORY OF LANDSCAPE DESIGN

The Touchstone of Design

When you approach your home after a trip out into the rest of the world, does the sight of your home invite you into a sanctuary, a retreat, a refuge from the cares of the world? When you are inside your home and looking out, do you find something beautiful, amusing and/or intriguing? When you walk around your property, are the areas you go to easy to approach, attractive, useful? If you have to answer "no" to any of these questions, it is time to take another look at landscapes—timeless landscapes—and see how you can put the lessons learned through hundreds of years to work outside your own door in a landscape that pleases the eye, nourishes the soul and makes living easier.

No property exists in a vacuum. Your landscape may be a chaotic mess, be frozen in stone or just need a tune-up. To separate the wheat from the chaff, designers use two main tools: art prin-ciples and a structured design process. The whole property can be treated at once or attention can be focused on each of the four parts: the approach and arrival sequence, the hub, the perimeter or passages to destinations.

In a timeless landscape design, a work of art springs directly from the potential revealed during the design process. Think of your property as a canvas with a design already started, which requires skillful editing. A set of environmental considerations and func-tional needs is already in place.

A background in historic models offers insight, so begin a design library of ways to treat the four inter-connected parts of the master plan. This philosophy will guide selection of the plant materials, hardscapes and landscape structures used to shape and accent spaces.

Abstract art principles will elegantly work hand in hand with the site's potentials and constraints once you know the language. The challenge is to learn to use these tools.

Curving borders beside it soften the tall, enclosing courtyard wall. The blue pot offers a colorful accent to the brown and green palette.

The approach and arrival sequence to this hub pays close attention to landscape and hardscape materials and knits the land to the house, resulting in a pleasing whole. Inward- and outward-looking views capture and empower your home.

RIGHT: Perimeter pathways often link grilling areas with entertainment zones, such as swimming pools and dining terraces.

To Create a Timeless Landscape

Gardens created 500 years ago still speak to us as places of unmistakable beauty as relevant today as ever before. Master plans evolve due to social and physical pressures and are today standard practice for design professionals. We call the process the Four-Part Master Plan to underscore that it is both a planning process and an end result.

The universal organization format for residential properties consists of four basic parts:

- **The Approach and Arrival Sequence** creates a presence for the house and a sense of anticipation leading up to the front entrance. It is the welcome mat to your property, announcing who you are and building interest in your home. The approach and arrival sequence takes you from the street to the front door.

- **The Hub** is the property's natural center. All functions occur around the hub, and from it, inward-

and outward-looking views capture and empower your home. Close attention to landscape and hardscape materials seamlessly integrates the house into its natural setting, resulting in a pleasing whole.

- **The Perimeter** consists of outdoor spaces wrapped tightly around the house opening from interior rooms and providing convenient and functional areas for dining, recreation, entertaining or simply sitting still. Here you can relax with friends, give a party or read a book and still be available to children, guests or what's cooking in the kitchen.

■ **Passages to Destinations** animate movement around a property and invite the enjoyment of garden places removed from the house. They are as important as any part of the planning process and streamline functional and aesthetic flow on the property. Destinations are varied and include kitchen gardens, ornamental pools, compost and potting areas, etc. Well-planned destinations and passages to them make it possible to enjoy all your property.

Properties well versed in these four components are particularly coherent, settled and at peace with themselves. They respond to basic human needs and evoke an aura of timelessness.

This concept is useful to you in planning a garden and developing your property. By dividing a property into these four components and their sub-components, by concentrating on each, one at a time, and by paying attention to how they interrelate, the design process settles down from chaos into something manageable and exhilarating.

By keeping these four parts firmly in your mind you can focus on a piece without losing sight of the whole. A successful home landscape is a seamless interconnection of spaces that is "of a piece."

The Four-Part Master Plan outlines landscape and outdoor spaces that are impeccably and imaginatively designed, that harmonize with the character of the house and site and express the owner's personality. The mission is to impart an aura of ageless beauty and a spirited sense of sophistication and individuality. Using the Four-Part Master Plan is a way to organize the creative process and structure your thinking.

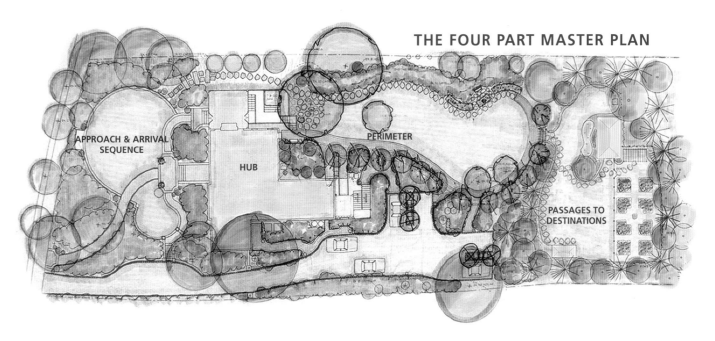

THE FOUR PART MASTER PLAN

APPROACH & ARRIVAL
SEQUENCE

HUB

PERIMETER

PASSAGES TO
DESTINATIONS

The Rest of the Story.

The Four-Part Master Plan is a philosophy of site structure from which design decisions emerge. However, an organizing principle by itself is not enough to create something of lasting interest. Three resources, or conceptual tools, guide the design process: 1) art elements and design principles, 2) the design process methodology and 3) historic patterns and *genius loci,* or *spirit.*

The **first** set of conceptual tools—the **art elements and design principles**—underlies the creation of all visual art and three-dimensional design. These basic tools of visual art—the four art elements (color, form, line and texture) and the broader principles of design, such as proportion, scale and focalization—are applied at each step of the planning process.

FACING: Line is one of the most easily recognized of the four art elements because it leads your eye into the landscape. Line often relates to pathways, which are easily designed to add interest to the landscape, as these curves do.

RIGHT: The process of design is a straightforward set of steps for planning and organizing your property. Rarely does a harmonious, well-connected landscape happen without a master plan providing a springboard for budgetary and long-range decisions. These elegant limestone, balustraded steps were coaxed into existence by first drawing elevations and sections from the plan that showed how they interconnected with the perimeter of the property.

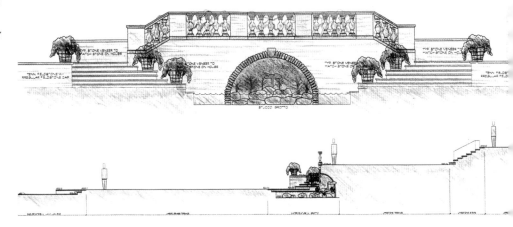

The **second** resource, **design process methodology**, features the mapping of the existing features of a site, analyzing the environmental constraints, defining your program or wish list for site uses and fitting these needs together into a seamless whole. This data collection provides the underpinnings for your design.

The phenomenon of **recognizing and honoring the genius loci** that resides in a particular site or place is the **third** resource. The quest for properties with a strong genius loci is a rich but elusive experience. With this concept planted firmly in our imaginations, we drew upon insight from nature and designed many of our favorite projects.

Seeking inspiration in the best examples of landscape architecture is essential to enriching one's powers of creative thinking and problem solving. Application of the Four-Part Master Plan is enriched through continual observations of superior examples. Taking photographs; sketching, and memorizing harmonious examples of seamless properties or artful compositions will develop your eye.

The Four-Part Master Plan
and Your Design

Later in this book, you will learn about each part of the Four-Part Master Plan and how to apply it. For now, do this:

- Make a notebook for yourself of beautiful places that you see and study them to see what makes them wonderful to you. You may not copy these places, but you might adapt them to your site.

- Look at the approach to the property, the way it is laid out, the plants that are used, the materials of walls and drive, and the lighting.

- Look at the house itself—the materials, colors and roof shape. See how it fits with the natural growth or the landscape on the property. Almost any house can be made to fit into the land with proper care—from a stately mansion to a small cabin, from a fifties ranch to a modern cube, and everything in between and on either side.

- Look at porches or terraces. Can you tell how they are to be used? Do they appear to be used at all? What makes them inviting—or the opposite? What makes them beautiful or compelling? You can use these same features for your perimeter areas.

- Look beyond the house. Are there buildings, features, gardens or pools farther away from the house? Study how they are accessed. The paths/walkways on a property can make the difference between dreading to go somewhere and going happily.

Make notes about the things that you find particularly attractive or successful and that strike the right note with you. Take pictures. Tear pictures from magazines and include them. Draw on these pictures or cut them up, if you want to. You are going to become a designer and you are beginning to develop your design.

In summary, the three design resources—art, design process and historic precedent—insure that the organization of your property is appealing in many ways and fits with the natural features of your property. The art resource provides a means to design a picture. The design process is a tool to bring this artistic picture to reality. History and genius loci identify your property's place in time and its unique qualities.

ABOVE: How does your property fit into the context of what man calls home? Not everyone has the opportunity to create a vista and water garden like this one at Buscot, a National Trust property in England, but you can certainly be inspired by the design. Studying garden design in situ or in books is a wonderful teaching tool. A pearl of design inspiration will provide enlightenment for you when you least expect.

LEFT: Certain places strike a chord that stays with you long after parting. Barnsley, under the tenancy of the late Rosemary Verey, did this for us. We learned about garden style, scale and personalization of spaces from a master. This sundial at Barnsley Gardens is 30" tall and is the focal point of a laburnam walk that is 8' wide.

The Tools of Landscape Design

The most important ingredients of a powerful landscape are usually not plants, flowers, buildings or trees. The key to success lies in the basic tools of visual art: the four art elements (line, color, form and texture) and the broader principles of design, such as proportion, scale and focalization. All gardens that have stood the test of time convey the power these tools hold over the human imagination. Crafting a four-part master plan depends on their skillful application–a lifelong pursuit. The following is a small taste of what these tools are and how they work on the land.

Art Elements.

Lines and Paths. Line commands power in landscape design because it not only gives form but also creates mood. Arrow-straight lines for pathways are purposeful; they propel you along with direct momentum. Curved paths relax the pace. On large properties, long, curving paths with tall shrubs and border plantings orchestrate the discovery of something hidden around the bend.

Hedges are lines; pleached alleys of trees are lines; the curvy or straight raised edges of flower beds are lines. They all create energy in the land-scape one way or another—through moving your eye or by moving your feet.

Line in a landscape is often implied. For exam-ple, a focal point such as a strategically placed arch can pull the eye along a straight trajectory into the distance with nothing on the ground plane reinforc-ing it.

An abundance of straight lines in a landscape design is a more formal and imposing atmosphere; repeated curves lend a more intimate and relaxed feeling. Contemporary and historic landscape designs find places for both.

Color. Color is the most personal part of a landscape design. Freedom of color choice rules your flower beds and borders, so you can choose to be over the top one year and restrained the next. As a tip, keep color simple. This applies to the plant color green as well as to the more vivid floral spectrums.

The backbone of any garden is green—blue green, leaf green, red green, variegated green or grass green. Take your choice. By merging and mingling greens, a garden can be as cool as a cucumber and as exciting as a Monet. Winter greens are different from summer greens. Gardens with year-round interest have both evergreen and deciduous plants. This lends considerable interest to spring when infant leaves burst forth from the sleeping gray branches.

A floral display that includes a palette ranging from dark to light will interest the eye. In a flower bed, you might try a dark blue theme with light blue, lavender and some pink for contrast, then add a dollop of pale yellow or white to release the colors and make the bed shimmer and twinkle. Successful beds showcase different hues that blend in with one another rather than stand out against each other. Try not to use independent wads of color such as tight clumps of bright begonias; instead, blend colors to luminously fade into one another like a watercolor.

Dark, shady places scream for flashes of light. To bring light into dark places, try the variegated foliage found in warmer climates: hydrangeas, hostas, fatsias, aspidistra or ligularias. These cream and soft green leaves create a soft foil for almost any other color nearby.

The color palette for flowers near the house draws its inspiration from the color of the architecture. Cool flower colors range from pale pinks and blues to purples and cream and look particularly good with frame and

stone houses. Warm-hued houses, like those of Mediterranean sepia stucco, look great with soft yellow, soft orange and cream with some medium blue added as a complement. This is a rich combination. Georgian brick companions well with salmon-colored tulips, bronze or grenadine chrysanthemums mixed with pale, yellow daisy mums, or dark violets and blues with a little pink. Brick is almost a neutral.

Bright and bold strokes, such as red geraniums in white containers displayed in a sun-drenched spot, might look great in the south of France, but sunlight might not be as kind in other places. Be careful not to overuse warm hues, for a garden can quickly get over-excited and harsh. Use red with success in a Red Hot Mama border and tone it down with vibrant purples and colorful foliage plants, like coleus, for a tropical summer feeling.

Monochromatic choices enlarge spaces and provide a feeling of calm. Limiting the color palette to a single cool or neutral hue—such as a gray blue—with subtle variations is often the best approach in a small, enclosed space, and it creates an elegant and refined look almost anywhere.

Form. Form means shape. Be it a rug of lawn or an upright conifer, the skillful use of form is a path to stylistic success in gardens, especially small spaces. Every element in a landscape has a form. Distinctive forms, such as Italian cypresses, have stylistic reasons for

being in gardens and evoke the flavor of Italy. The contours of a shapely lawn, the graceful outline of a large stone urn, or tall boxwoods clipped into whimsical bird-like topiaries demonstrate the variable art element of form.

Plant materials offer you choices in forms that include horizontal, vertical, loose (billowing), tight (compact), weeping, upright, pyramidal, clasping, curving, linear, asymmetrical and symmetrical.

Cemeteries often showcase forms that are elongated (e.g., tall conifers) and have an inspirational or serene effect. They lead your eye skyward. Wider forms, such as low, clipped boxwood hedges, bring you back to earth and emphasize the ground plane. Irregular forms, such as Deodar cedar, are picturesque. Your eye sees the irregular voids between the branches.

Texture. Understanding texture is akin to pouring soy milk into a bowl of granola. At first glance, it is a pebbly surface full of interest; the next moment it is a broad expanse of flatness with an occasional iceberg. Textures in the landscape represent the symbiotic relationship between plant leaf sizes, the size of the space in which they are placed and any adjacent paving textures.

In plant materials, there are three basic textural categories: large, medium and fine. Large-leaved plants, such as fatsia, banana trees, palmettos, magnolias, hydrangeas and

hostas, are considered coarse. Fine textures are seen in grasses (especially zoysia) and plants with dainty leaves, such as creeping fig vine, small leaf hollies and small ferns. Medium textures would be exhibited by camellia, azalea indica, ivy and cherry laurel. Some plants may have a specific texture but read more as shape. Boxwood is considered to have fine texture, but that is usually not as important as its form when used in a design.

Textures play a major role in all of the built elements in a garden, be it stone or brick. A path made out of a single smooth surface and hue, such as square limestone paving stones with closely mortared joints, creates momentum, this effect is doubled when the path follows a straight line. On the other hand, a heavier, coarser texture, such as bricks laid in a basket-weave pattern, slow it down. Using the heavier texture on a curved path definitely puts on the brakes and seems to invite relaxation.

Keeping the textures of building materials and plant materials in the same general family defines the character of a property. Skillful use of texture is one of the most powerful elements you have for creating a spirit of place. Each building material and individual plant has its own expressive surface. For example, the coarse texture of weathered cedar used on fences and gates in a mountain retreat differs from a town courtyard garden where a smoother texture of painted ironwork, stucco or wood would be more appropriate.

Principles of Design

Great gardens have a secret language. Their hidden underpinnings are design principles. This lexicon is critical to your success as a designer. With these words, you can describe why a garden visually works.

Axial Relationships. An axis is simply a straight line, like a path or an alley of trees, extending from a starting point to an ending point that's usually punctuated with a visual element such as a building or fountain at the end. Intersecting the line with another one, at right angles, produces cross-axial design. Few other visual techniques produce

such a strong grip on the landscape. With this elegantly simple device, many wildernesses have been tamed and many gardens given their structural bones.

Cross-axial design created the shape of the cloister garden in medieval monasteries. A walled space was divided into four sections by two intersecting paths. A fountain, well, basin or tree was usually placed at the center point, or node, where the two paths crossed; in the four resulting planting beds, the monks tended fruit trees, herbs and flowers.

Beginning in the seventeenth century in Europe and England, four planting beds—or the four-square form—created by the intersection of two paths became the standard plan for kitchen gardens. Its application continues to this day, and we often find a place for it in landscape designs in a variety of settings.

Both axial and cross-axial designs suggest rationality and spatial discipline. When used within a small walled space, such as the cloister or kitchen garden, they create a calmly ordered and balanced environment. When let loose on a very grand scale, axial and cross-axial designs become extremely powerful psychologically because they seem to dominate nature. In the seventeenth century, for example, axial design structured vast properties that underscored the

FACING: Pathways often bisect and form a node, which is a decision-making element in the landscape. A straight line is an axis along which other elements are arranged. A cross-axial relationship is illustrated by this garden node in Sissinghurst in England.

LEFT: When an axis, or straight line, terminates in a landscape, the eye continues until stopped by trees or a hedge or drifts on to the horizon beyond. This focal point is well placed at the end of a visual axis in this garden in Charleston, South Carolina.

where else, along an axis, or at its end point. While, for example, a jungle gym may be peripherally in sight, its impact is considerably lessened when a strong axial statement is taking place somewhere in the opposite direction.

Formality often implies axial and cross-axial design; therefore, in the vast majority of cases, paths in a formal flower garden are predominantly straight lines. Cross-axial designs are used to create parterres for flower gardens and kitchen gardens on properties of all styles and sizes. The four-square form is one of the most beautiful and enduring of all landscape designs. Variations on this form abound through the crafting of differently shaped beds; they don't have to be rectangular or square.

Focalization. Focalization is a technique for making order out of chaos by providing a focal point that funnels the viewer's sight line where you want it to go. A statue, pergola or garden gate can each be used to create a strong focus. Something as simple as an urn or birdbath in direct line with the back door is elemental focalization. An entire composition can be created around it.

Focalization also implies using a framing device, such as a rounded arch, to isolate and emphasize a particular sight line or view. This technique has been used masterfully by architects and landscape architects from time immemorial.

Focalization is almost always an ingredient in axial and cross-axial design. An "exclamation point" such as a statue, urn or tree at the end of an axis becomes a focal point that draws the eye.

In small spaces, we sometimes increase the illusion of space by making things seem smaller or closer together as they near the focal point, mimicking the effect of visual perspective and the way things get smaller as they go into the distance. This can be used effectively in small courtyard gardens in which a wall provides the backdrop for a focal point such as a piece of sculpture or a fountain, and the entire composition is organized around that single element.

power of their owners; the longer and straighter the lines, the greater the sense of domination, power and authority. The gardens created for Louis XIV at Versailles are the ultimate example.

In addition to making a small space crisp and thus visually larger, axial design can divert attention away from an unattractive area on a property by whisking the eye toward a visual element such as an arch or arbor placed some-

Symmetry and Asymmetry. Chaos and order. Be it a house or landscape under construction, chaos results. Even the most ordered man-made landscape in picturesque or formal style goes through a learning curve involving earth moving and revegetation. A master landscape plan helps navigate the rough road to perfection. Look to Mother Nature for clues involving environmental concerns to make the ultimate landscape ordered by both man and natural processes.

In landscape design, symmetry refers to a method of placing shapes of equal volume, size or form on either side of a central point or along an axis. What is on the left side is mirrored on the right. Symmetrically placed forms add stability and balance.

The formal gardens of the geometric period in France in the seventeenth century were founded on symmetrical design. The picturesque English landscape gardens of the eighteenth century reacted against it and celebrated the naturalness of asymmetry. In contemporary residential landscape design, we often combine elements of symmetry and asymmetry in different parts of the master plan to achieve formality, informality or, as is often the case, a subtle blending of both.

Repetition and Rhythm. When a similar form is repeated at regular or irregular intervals, a certain rhythm results. Bouncing balls of boxwoods have delighted generations of gardeners and are probably one of the most vivid examples of repetition. When similar forms are organized in a single direction, the effect of rhythmic movement is even stronger. The technique of repeating the same shape gives a landscape design a feeling of unity; the

eye seems to like the echoing of a form, and we subconsciously join these elements together into a whole scene. The use of large, repeated forms, such as clipped cedars, takes a bit of conviction because its effect tends to dominate. When done well, few design treatments have more authority or sophistication.

Light and Shadow. Going along with color, light and shadow playing off one another has its own emotive language. Dappled light filtering onto a lawn or forest floor creates an ever-changing wash of patterns. An environment like this releases you from prosaic thoughts and evokes a feeling of serenity and inspiration. The animated light quality reduces the feeling of enclosure and encourages peaceful thought.

Proportion and Scale. Most of the western world's greatest architectural achievements demonstrate a mastery of proportion (i.e., the relationship of parts to the whole). In architecture, proportion has been traditionally founded in the rigors of mathematics and geometry. This is why geniuses like Andrea Palladio in the Renaissance took the trouble to learn the numerical proportions of the Roman builders.

The more formal designs in landscape architecture also have their historical roots in classical proportions, although now they are rarely taught. For most landscape architects working on residential projects, determining proportion is largely a matter of sensing and intuiting, through training one's eye, how to create harmonious spatial relationships between the parts of a design and the whole. If you study the most renowned sites and clas-

sic examples of architecture and landscape design, you will internalize a feeling for proportional relationships that look and feel right. Scale relates a bit more to the size of elements in relationship to their context. *Out of scale* refers to an overly large object placed in a too-small setting. *Under-scaled* is a tiny object lost in an ocean of space like an acorn on a lawn. In general, we find that people tend to under-scale statuary and pots in relation to where they are being

used. For those two categories of objects, we tend to advise, "When in doubt, select a more generous rather than a smaller size." This is especially true of pots.

Reflection. When there is a possibility of using it, reflection adds depth and a sense of mystery to a scene. The reflection of light across water draws the eye and makes a space lively in the sunshine and soothing in the evening. Trees beside a pool seem taller and assume more importance. The effect of color is doubled.

The creative use of the tools of visual art lies in designing a visually stimulating landscape using the four art elements (line, color, form and texture) and the broader principles of design such as proportion, scale and focalization. By visiting notable landscapes, photographing, sketching and studying the plans, you will build a strong foundation for your design.

ABOVE: Repetition of urn and plant forms in the Laskett, Sir Roy Strong's garden in England, leads the eye from Tatiana's Walk to the Beaton Sundial through the Silver Jubilee garden and terminating at the John Taylor monument and Triumphal Arch in the Rose Garden.

Applying Graphic Elements of
Art and Design Principles

Line

Line is often hidden or elusive in a landscape due to random placement of plant materials and differing notes of paving. Study a photograph of your property and trace the line of the walk, the line of hedge and any other line. What changes could you make to create a more pleasing composition based on this art element?

Color

The color green offers a calming foil for a riot of flowers or can be enjoyed as a study of subtle hues from pale mint to dark evergreen. A good way to experiment with green is to purchase a handful of magic art markers or colored pencils, go to a nursery and try to copy the colors of the leaves into a sketchbook.

Form

Try experimenting with forms by placing a piece of transparent paper over this photo and tracing the dominant forms. This composition comes from The Old Rectory in Norfolk, England. Do the same with a photo of your own property.

Texture

The illusion of airiness in a tiny, walled courtyard is extended by installing fine-textured cobblestones against coarser textured paving slabs of crab orchard stone. Point of view and perspective guide all planting designs. Objects in the foreground of a composition look larger than those behind. Experiment with making an area feel closer by planting it with heavier textures.

Axial Relationships

A cross axis denotes a node, or place for decision-making, in the land. At Sissinghurst, in England, the circular hedging with four entry points is a classic example of a node at a major cross axis. Look for nodes on your property; they need not be as formal as this one. Often the "problems are all in your nodes."

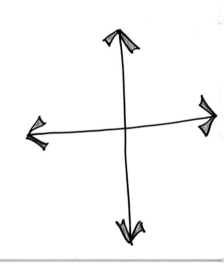

Focalization

A strategically placed sculpture terminates the long, straight walk in this Huntsville, Alabama, garden. Focal points strengthen an axial view. Look for focal points or places where they could be crafted on your own property. A focal point can be something as simple as a bench or a pot or as fine as a lovely piece of statuary or a custom-made fountain.

Light & Shadow

Light and shadow provide a dimension in landscape design that is not often planned. Look at your designs at all times of day and seasons; the changing light will enliven pavement or offer a cool retreat when least expected. At La Fronteira Palace in Lisbon, Portugal, this strong shadow form occurred in mid-winter.

Symmetry & Asymmetry

Balance is synonymous with symmetry and is a hallmark of formal gardens. Occult balance, or asymmetry, is often found in gardens with an Asian influence or in contemporary art. Both Hidcote Gardens in England and Medway (at left) in the United States illustrate balanced plans aligned on a central axis. Even in a small or informal garden there can be an area of symmetry. Look at your own garden with this in mind. Would a symmetrical composition add to the feeling that you want? Would asymmetry be better for your landscape?

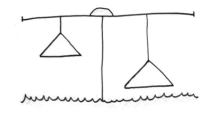

Repetition & Rhythm

Repetition usually works with the art elements of line and form by multiplying the initial effort. In this Charleston, South Carolina, garden, the jets of water splash an outline of the pool coping and energize the environment with the rhythm of the water movement and sound. Repetition and rhythm can also be found in plantings and in the architecture of structures. Look for these elements in your landscape. Sometimes even small changes can make a big difference.

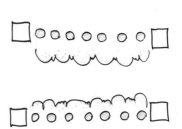

Proportion & Scale

Mocking up full-scale models is very useful in testing scale. This Huntsville, Alabama, garden benefited from careful analysis of the scale and placement of a number of urns. The proper scale can make the difference between an outstanding arrangement and one that always looks a little "off."

Reflection

Reflection, like light and shadow, is elusive. Generations of designers have used reflection to great effect to empower a house, such as this magnificent reflection at Melbourne in England. A simple dark-bottomed pool or birdbath can provide a reflective surface.

Chaos & Order

Man molds nature to his purposes by levelling land, making pathways, building houses and planting gardens. This process is complex. Without a good plan, it is challenging to build a landscape. During the construction process, order becomes chaos then returns to order. Much like tossing a pebble into a still body of water, a landscape under change sends out shock waves until is it calmed by the final design complete with mulch, ground cover and restorative plant material.

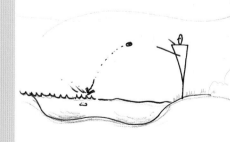

LEFT: This sunken court-
yard design in Charleston,
South Carolina, went
through the steps of the
design process. A set of
plans was created to guide
the implementation process.
The space is 20' x 20' and
tentable for parties.

RIGHT: The undulating
length of lawn interests the
eye and visually expands
the property. At its narrowest
point, the garden is 6' wide
and 60' long.

The Design Process

The Master Plan involves the organization of outdoor space. Properties that look right
usually work well for the owners. They are seamless, beautiful and intangibly functional.
But how do you go about effecting the improvement of your inadequately designed or
nonfunctional home grounds?

The organization of outdoor space has three
givens. These are the size and location of the
house, the configuration of the grounds and
desires of the owner. But first you need to have well-
defined goals for all parts of your property. A Master
Plan is easily divided into four parts: the Approach and
Arrival Sequence, the Hub or house, the Perimeter and
Passages to Destinations. Record a wish list for future
improvements for each of the four sections, but keep
the big picture in mind. In this way you can pay attention
to details in list form, refer to them in your site analysis
and later transfer them onto a base sheet.

These guidelines are the pathway to landscape
design and are intended to structure your decision-making
process, not to bog you down! Consider this an opportunity to become a designer with foresight. By following a
design process with a functional and artistic structure, the
improvement of your site is logical and orderly.

There are twelve steps to the design process to guide each landscape design.

- Make a survey
- Develop a base plan
- Inventory the site
- Analyze the site
- Develop a program wish list
- Create a functional diagram
- Develop a concept diagram
- Sketch alternative plans
- Verify field conditions
- Create a master landscape plan
- Make implementation drawings
- Get it built

An overlay system whereby different levels of information are drawn on semitransparent tissue paper in order to view layers of information beneath is a useful tool.

The survey is the basis for your future master plan. Accuracy is important. A survey is a plan of your property showing existing trees and shrub masses, topography and the future or existing location of a house and drive. It records boundary and easement facts in graphic form. A survey from a licensed surveyor is worth its weight in gold. However, it is also possible to make your own plan.

Making Your Own Survey and Base Plan. Find your plat and architectural drawings from a surveyor or on file in the deed record room at the county courthouse. Study them.

- Make an enlargement of the plat or the garden area at a blueprint shop (use 1/8" or 1/4"=1'-0"); get three copies—one on vellum and two on bond (blueprint).
- Purchase an architectural scale and a roll of tracing paper (available at office supply stores).
- Rent a 100' or 200' engineer's tape at the printer store (can be purchased at a hardware store).
- Measure and record everything related to

your garden area (this includes the house, trees, paving and power). Measure from property lines, if possible.
- Sketch your measurements on one of the blueprints; transfer data to scale on second blueprint copy later.
- Label everything on your drawing.
- Find north and show the direction with an arrow (this is useful for site analysis and shade patterns).
- Write the scale you are using on the map, i.e., 1/8"=1' (three months later you will have forgotten!).
- Overlay and trace from blueprint onto the original vellum and get another print (the base sheet).
- Before and after photos: It is critical that you take "head-on" and panoramic views of your property. These early photos provide a platform for sketching new ideas.

The site analysis records the constraints and potentials of your property posed by

Topography

Simple changes in elevation are represented on topographic maps. Contour lines represent 1', 2', 5', 10' or 100' changes in elevation between the lines. A swale, creek or river is shown as a dash and dotted line, which crosses contour lines as it runs downhill.

RIGHT: A plat shows the property line, the house and drive, the north arrow, the scale, the easements, the setback lines and the surveyor's stamp.

Applying Graphic **Elements** of **Art and Design Principles**

Blank canvas

Test of Scale Statue

Final Landscape

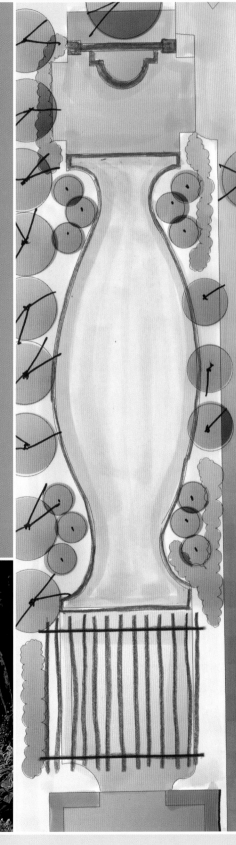

Create a baby book of your garden's progress by taking before, during and after photographs. This garden in Charleston, South Carolina, was a rectilinear lawn with uninspired plantings. The garden is very small and narrow, only twenty feet wide and sixty feet long. The owners wanted curves and art forms, so we tested the scale of the statue and added curves for a sense of perspective, plus an arbor. Voila!

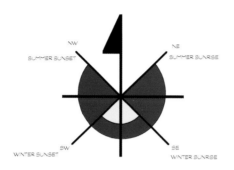

SUN DIAGRAM

TOP: This diagram shows where the sun will rise and set throughout the year.

MIDDLE: Site analysis.

BELOW: A series of sketches that show proposed and existing pathways on your property will identify functional problem areas.

FACING TOP: An architect's scale is a useful measuring tool for house plans and home landscapes. Larger properties use an engineer's scale.

FACING MIDDLE: Frequently used equipment for drawing plans includes a circle template, triangle and scale.

FACING BELOW: An architect's scale is vital for measuring small amounts of footage.

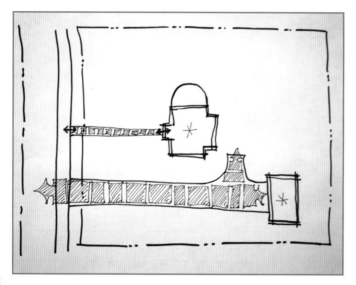

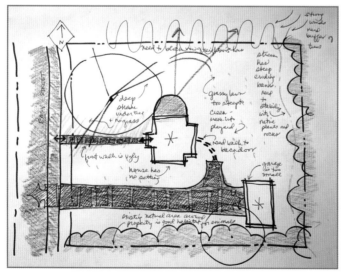

existing environmental and functional considerations and helps you determine your spirit of place. Keep the four parts of the master plan in mind as you analyze the property. When you survey the existing conditions, consider environmental constraints (topography, soils, vegetation and climate) as well as subjective ones (views). Include drainage problems, erosion, shade or lack of shade, individual plant problems, lack of order, etc. Site potentials are constructive observations made after thoughtful appraisal of your grounds, the wish list and your long-range plans. Determine the fall of the land by using a sight level and a ten-foot length of PVC pipe. If the land is too steep or if there are large numbers of trees, hire a professional. Label everything on the drawing, being sure that you note the scale you are using, and insert a north arrow. Include the items that are on your wish list by writing them on the plan copy where they would occur. This system is a reality check.

Nodes occur where functional or perceptual changes in function occur in the landscape. They are places of transition between one activity and another. Identification of nodes results in solving most of the functional problems on your property and improving the transitional sequence—paving, shade or ornamental plantings, gateways, walls and places to sit and wait. An overlay of semitransparent tissue on your survey provides a base for making little circles where two paths cross (such as the walk to the front door and the path from the street). Study this drawing to determine how an area can be tightened up or made into a real place.

To study functional outdoor spaces, put tracing paper over your base plan and draw dashed lines around places where different functions occur. Draw an entry arrow. This is the linkage passage to a destination. It can be

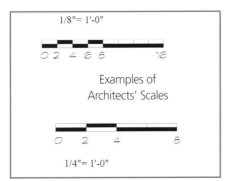

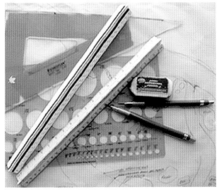

Examples of
Architects' Scales

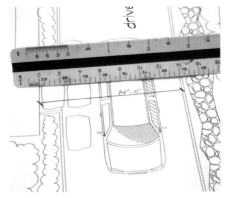

as simple as a walk to the trash can. Each functional outdoor space offers potential for the skillful application of the art elements and design principles. Adjust this until it is right according to the analysis you did earlier. Remember to take into account the views to and from the house.

Mechanics of Delineation. Drafting skills are needed to execute reproducible, scaled drawings for construction and planning purposes. These skills involve mechanical equipment such as pencils of varying lead thicknesses, triangles, a straight edge or parallel bar, circle guides, eraser and an architect's or an engineer's scale or a computer assisted drafting program. Of the equipment, the scales are most important, for they allow for varying details to be accurately drawn.

Accuracy in conveying the design intent for any spot on the master plan is crucial in getting it built correctly. You will need some practice in switching from scale to scale, but once mastered, you will find it indispensable.

An architect's scale shows in fractions of the inch (i.e., 1/4"=1'-0", 1/2"=1'-0"). These sizes are well adapted to showing details on drawings such as brick borders or intricate perennial planting arrangements.

An engineer's scale shows in tenths (i.e., 1"=20', 1"=60'). It can also be read as 1"=200' or 1"=600', or even 1"=2' or 1"=6'. It is most useful in showing a large property in its entirety.

Symbols for Delineation. Plant materials (i.e., shrubs, ground covers, trees, existing and proposed plantings) are all shown as symbols that represent the size of the proposed plant material at ten to fifteen years of age and the existing plant materials as accurately as possible.

Symbols for these materials are shown

as circles and are measured according to the scale of the drawing. If a tree is estimated to be twenty feet in diameter at ten to fifteen years of age, then a drawing at 1"=20' will show this tree circle to be one inch in diameter. These tree circles are carefully spaced around the drawing according to the constraints of the site, the designer's intentions and the budget of the owner. The same principle relates to shrubs and smaller trees. It is important to have a circle guide to delineate mature tree sizes.

Ground covers are graphically shown as slashed lines or as dots connected with lines, and a suggested spacing will be included on the plant materials schedule. Label all plants on the planting plan, whether existing or proposed, using a leader and arrow technique.

When drawing trees, note the diameter of the trunk at breast height (DBH) in inches, plus the type of tree. Depict this diameter as actual size to scale, then determine the extent of the canopy, which will be this number x2 in feet. It will look enormous, but rest assured it is correct. This is why you have shade.

Plant Inventory. Inventory the plants existing on your property, measuring the space they occupy. Draw them on the proper place on your plan using a circle guide.

The garden matrix is a conceptual four-sided box that prompts you to fully consider all possibilities in your designs. Scale of the garden environment, the soil conditions, seasonal change and design considerations all play an overlapping role in a well-expressed landscape.

Types of Design Documents. Design documents are packages of individual sheets typically bound together as a plan package. These are used to obtain cost estimates from the contractor and for him to accurately construct his portion of the work according to the design. Construction plans are legally binding documents and contain enough detail to allow the contractor to execute his job with a minimum amount of observation or inspection by the consultant or owner.

A complete set of construction drawings for landscape typically consists of the following individual sheets: title sheet, site plan, master plan, layout plan, grading plan, material reference, planting plan and construction details. These sheets are bound together as a set when issued to a general landscape contractor. On occasion, individual sheets are given to the skilled workmen involved with planting, carpentry,

RIGHT: The 2x4 Plant Inventory. A list of plants using the 2x4 method (2=evergreen and deciduous, 4=trees, shrubs, ground covers, vines and ephemerals) reminds you to design in a layered way, using a palette of plants from tall shade trees to the minutiae of ground covers. If you provide interest in your garden using these parameters, success will be yours.

PLANT LIST MATRIX				
	TREES	SHRUBS	GROUND COVERS	ANNUALS
SMALL				
MEDIUM				
LARGE				
WET				
DRY				
SUNNY				
SPRING				
SUMMER				
FALL				
WINTER				

masonry or grading of the land. Another document, the specifications booklet, is issued to further instruct the contractors about engineering standards, scheduling work and payment procedures.

Descriptions of the individual sheets are as follows:

The title sheet lists the address of the project and the name of the owner. The name, address and phone number of the landscape architecture firm is included on this sheet plus the date the drawings were completed. A list of sheets and their titles are listed in a table of contents.

The site master plan delineates the location and specific boundaries of the design area. All built features such as buildings, roadways, walkways, parking areas, planting areas, drainage basins and suggested focal points appear on this sheet. Each sheet in a set of drawings includes a directional North arrow, scale, sheet title,

date and the name, address and phone number of the designer or design firm.

The layout, or staking plan, provides all dimensions necessary to lay out a design on a site. Construction details are referenced to enlargements on this drawing and include considerably more information. The point of beginning (POB) is typically shown on the staking plan to enable a systematic location or layout of each proposed feature.

The grading plan is used by both masonry and earth-working contractors. It provides elevations necessary to properly cut or fill a site by showing spot elevations and contours. The intent is to show the difference in elevation between the existing features and proposed construction. Drainage patterns, berms and catch basins and underground pipes are referenced to construction details.

Planting plans feature locations for existing and proposed plant materials and a schedule of plants to be installed. The plant

materials schedule contains the genetic and common names of selected plants, size of container and caliper of tree, notes concerning special plants and the numbers of specific types of plants required. Planting plans are used for cost estimating and communicating design intent.

Construction around existing trees is tricky. The drip line shown on the survey is a very fragile zone. The tree protection plan shows fencing that extends to the edge of the drip line or at least twenty feet from the trunk. The best type of tree protection is chain-link fence that is rented for the duration of the project. Other types of fencing are easily destroyed by construction mishaps. It is important to protect the active root zone from compaction; under no circumstances allow trucks or heavy equipment to park within the root zone. If access must be made through a woodland, provide a specification for six inches of mulch as a running path. Trees suffering from compaction die a slow death up to three to five years after the instance.

Other plans indicate site furnishings and systems. A lighting plan provides all details necessary to properly light a garden, including a schedule of fixtures. The irrigation plan features all piping and sleeves necessary to provide site coverage with water, plus a schedule of fixtures. A furniture plan provides all details necessary to properly furnish and pot a garden, including a schedule of fixtures.

Construction details are drawings that enlarge specific site features to enable the contractor to know the exact size, color, finish and grade of materials. Every sheet in a design document package may contain construction details or reference the majority of them to individual sheets that show the details necessary to execute construction.

10' RADIUS

20' CANOPY

10" CALIPER TREE
AT BREAST HEIGHT

1/4"=1'0"

2' 4'   8'   16'

GUIDELINES FOR PROTECTING TREE ROOTS:

- Change number of caliper inches to feet
- Number of feet equals radius from trunk to edge of root protection

LEFT: Quick sketches on photographs will often help you test new design ideas.

Large projects require city and county permits. Permit drawing sets typically include a location map and site survey, a demolition plan and haul route, cut and fill calculations and grading plan, sewer location, erosion control details, stamped engineer's retaining wall drawings and a tree replacement plan. These plans are prepared by licensed landscape architects or civil engineers.

Drawing a line on a blank piece of paper during the design process is daunting. A simple method for breaking into drafting is to simply draw to scale the longest line you have on the property, making it align with the edge of your paper. From this line measure the offsets that locate each tree or built feature. A licensed surveyor can really be your friend during this phase and can ensure that the base sheet with which you are struggling is correct.

Verifying Field Conditions. It is important to test your design on the site before you complete the drawings. Nothing is more disheartening or potentially expensive than incorrect or sloppy drawings in the hands of a contractor. The expense of undoing a construction mistake is enormous compared to taking a few hours to ensure that drawings are correct.

By ensuring that your drawings are complete enough, another person should understand your design intent. Keep in mind the artists' and designers' tools from chapter 2 and sketch alternative plans until you have your working plan. Verify by measuring and marking on the ground that your plan will work. Transfer the final plan to your vellum copy and have another copy made. This is your finished master plan.

Designing a Four-Part Master Plan can be a lengthy process but one that pays great rewards.

The Program Wish List

The program wish list is a preliminary set of personal guidelines for activities and places you'd like to include on your property. Just write what you want to do on the site, roughly on the spot where you wish it to occur. This preliminary program guides the design process. Examples include an addition to your house, a new garage, parking, a pool or a great lawn for play. The process is organized by dividing the plan into the four parts of the master plan and making a list for each part.

Historic Sources for Design Inspirations

Our pilgrimages to places recognized as masterpieces of landscape design began long before Hugh and I knew one another. We each discovered our own mentors and inspirations as students and young designers. After we married, the rate and intensity of our travels really took off. It began with our wedding trip to England, where we visited forty-two gardens in seven days.

The reason for this passion for travel was to discover the secrets of great properties. Even the best academic programs in landscape architecture play down residential projects and encourage students to concentrate on community planning and large-scale design. We chose a vocation and a tradition that required learning its nuances largely on our own, and we wanted to study firsthand from the best examples we could find.

Each great site has an underlying message if you dig deeply enough. Sometimes the message is about color and design; sometimes it is about an ambience and a genius loci almost sacred; sometimes it is about the courage to clearly imprint a personality on a site. Once in a while, in one little corner of a great property, it's about what not to do.

Photographs from many diverse and well-loved sites appear throughout the following chapters; here are some that made deep and lasting impressions on us. These gardens will inspire the reader to pluck pieces from history to apply to their own landscape and give direction to their design. Universal concepts from these landscapes are uniquely applicable to modern designers despite size and monumentality.

FACING: Color, line, tex-
ture and form all con-
tribute to the beauty of
this garden in Hidcote,
England. The topiary birds
add a whimsical note, and
the fountain and gate in
the far hedge lead our eye
into the distance.

Great Britain. The gardens of England, Scotland and Wales hold endless design lessons. In addition to the sites and garden designers mentioned, the English landscape architect Russell Page merits special mention. His book, *The Education of a Gardener*, had a profound impact on us. The work of Sir Edwin Lutyens (in collaboration with Gertrude Jekyll) fed our design sensibilities—especially his circular steps. Hugh Johnson's *The Principles of Gardening* stood out as perhaps the best explanation of art elements and design principles and reinforced our belief in their importance.

HIDCOTE MANOR & GARDEN, CHIPPING CAMDEN, GLOUCESTERSHIRE

Hidcote is a masterpiece of garden design created by the enigmatic horticulturalist Major Lawrence Johnston during the first half of the twentieth century around his Tudor-style house in the Cotswolds. Sited on a windy hill, it unfolds as a series of powerfully articulated garden enclosures delineated with walls and tall hedges of holly, copper beach, hornbeam and yew.

"Hidcote blue" is famous. It gave us the idea of permanent color that is year-round and is accented by plant materials. This notion was reinforced in Portugal and at The Laskett. Hidcote also excels in the creation of vistas and inward views—two techniques we cover in our discussion of the hub—and in utilizing the view beyond the enclosed spaces of the gardens. Its level of horticulture is unsurpassed, with borders in theme colors, hidden rooms, the use of form, repetition and focalization.

THE LASKETT, HEREFORDSHIRE

The Laskett is seldom open to the public. Sir Roy Strong and his wife, the late Dr. Julia Trevelyan Oman, shared their work of art with us. Begun in 1973 on a leftover field between two lanes, it now has thirty different garden rooms, making it one of the largest formal gardens created in Britain in the second half of the twentieth century.

But size is not what makes The Laskett unforgettable. It is a garden made by two incredibly erudite and talented individuals. Sir Roy, a scholar and writer, was formerly the director of the Victoria and Albert Museum in London and is an expert on garden history. Julia Trevelyan Oman is remembered as an internationally renowned set designer. The garden rooms that have slowly evolved from the starting point of their blue and yellow house tell a series of stories about their lives. Architectural fragments, flower beds, knot gardens, small buildings and pavilions are layered with clues. The Cecil Beaton steps, slate medallions with inscriptions, an epitaph here, a Latin phrase there, and the careful placement of gifts from friends all hint at deeper meanings and milestones in their lives.

The Laskett is a confirmation of everything we love. Its elegant garden rooms are pure expressions of artistic principles such as balance, repetition, rhythm, focalization and light and shadow. It embedded in our minds the importance of personalizing places; to this day we question clients to find out what their gardens will mean to them, and we look for ways to imprint their personalities in the project. Finally, as the creation of two artists with huge imaginations but less-than-limitless budgets, The Laskett is also > *54*

La Fronteira Palace, Lisboa, Portugal.

Over time, man designed landscapes with many stylistic variations. The Romans, known for world conquests, imposed their ideas on nature. Records from Pompeii show exquisite gardens in murals.

The Portuguese culture in the sixteenth and seventeenth centuries produced unrivaled excellence in beautiful furnishings, homes and opulent gardens. *Azulejos,* or painted tiles applied to surfaces of garden walls and seats, tell stories of the family's political conquests. Spanish gardens, similar in style, featured a water tank or basin, walls with *azulejos,* a green backbone, connection with the house, beautiful pots and well-placed citrus.

Over time, the Italians gained wealth and showed it by improving land. Two major periods of Italian gardens evolved: the Renaissance and Baroque. The architecture of Andrea Palladio, noted for respecting genius loci, played a part in the development of later styles. Hallmarks of Renaissance gardens are fountains, geometric layout, grottoes, masks, mythological statues and mazes.

The Baroque gardens include elaborate gateways/gatescreens, *acqua d'gnocci* (water jets) and overscaled plants and grottoes. Soaring Italian cypress, *Cupressus sempervirens,* are integral to all Italian garden designs.

The Courts, England.   Valsanzibio, Italy.

Villandry, France.

Not to be outdone by the Italians, the French, with lands owned by Louis XIV, the Sun King, crystallized the geometric landscape movement. The genesis of this new landscape movement sprang from the pen of Andre Le Notre, the designer of many properties for the Sun King. Hallmarks of French gardens are outward-facing views to the horizon, clipped geometric forms of plant materials, flat planes of terraced land, formal water bodies and canals—all of which illustrate man's sweeping dominance of the land.

French gardens remind us to "think outside the box" while reaching into the past for inspiration. They illustrate a continuum of layers of garden design with Fontainebleau and Vaux-le-Vicomte being the purest forms of geometric period landscape.

During the Age of Enlightenment, English noblemen undertook the Grand Tour and visited French and Italian museums, historic houses and seats of power. The concept of "spirit of place," *genius loci*, a reference to the Italian gods who live on the land, was embraced by these enlightened travelers. England, with its rolling hills and pastoral settings, embraced a natural picturesque landscape ethic, as opposed to the now-outdated geometric overlay. Jean Jacques Rousseau's (1712–78) visions captured the political symbolism of the era, which is unique in garden history. British landscape gardens featured grottoes, cascades, wild scenery and temples resem-

Stourhead, England.

bling a romantic landscape painting. William Hogarth, Alexander Pope and William Kent represented the cognoscenti of the period by popularizing the "line of beauty," a curvilinear artistic form that became the icon of the Picturesque landscape movement.

By the third quarter of the eighteenth century, American cities such as New York, Boston and Charleston had developed from pioneer outposts into centers of culture. Landscape designs reflected the owner's heritage, whether Italian, French, Portuguese, English or Spanish. Contemporary garden books often copied European texts. Thus, American designers adapted picturesque and geometric landscape styles to their properties. Designers, including presidents George Washington and Thomas Jefferson, used both styles to empower their properties.

Today, antique garden books such as those in the Cherokee Garden Library at the Atlanta History Center or at Dumbarton Oaks in Washington, D.C., provide a snapshot of our forefathers' gardens. The Garden Conservancy promotes conservation of built works of art. The Garden Club of America and the Historic American Landscape Survey (HALS) encourage conservation of garden heritage works on paper.

RIGHT: Cheekwood in Nashville, Tennessee, is an outstanding example of the Italian landscape tradition, executed with native plants such as Eastern Red Cedar (*Juniperus* virginia), instead of Italian cypress.

about experimentation and clever solutions to fashioning garden ornaments that look like the real thing but aren't. Read Sir Roy's book, *Ornament in the Garden,* for specific examples and for his own rich descriptions of creating this spirited place.

Sissinghurst Castle Garden, Sissinghurst, Kent

Sissinghurst, the life's work of Vita Sackville-West and her husband, Sir Harold Nicholson, feels layered by centuries of time but is a twentieth-century garden designed as a collection of enclosures laid out around the surviving parts of an Elizabethan mansion. Vita Sackville-West's prodigious knowledge of plants and her taste for intimate spaces led to each "room" having a specific theme built up with color and unerring plant associations. A tower remnant of the original Elizabethan mansion allows you to study the layout of the garden from a bird's-eye view and to absorb the exquisite sense of space, proportion and design. For us, Sissinghurst is one of the best places to study color and layers of ever-changing seasonal interest as well as all the design principles and art elements used to develop the genius loci.

Stourhead, near Warminster, Wiltshire

Stourhead is a vast eighteenth-century picturesque landscape built around a Georgian Palladian house that immediately fades away when you reach the end of the drive due to the powerfully seductive beauty of the grounds. An afternoon's stroll around this timeless paradise takes you on a circuit walk

around a man-made lake. It's an experience filled with surprise glimpses of perfectly sited classical temples, a fabulous grotto and majestically mature trees. One of the major impressions we took away from Stourhead was the use of iconographic meaning in the landscape, the power of a circular walk and the assured use of architectural elements as focal points in the landscape.

Barnsley House, Gloucestershire

It would be impossible to calculate how many thousands of people Rosemary Verey's gardening books and lectures had affected by the time she passed away in 2001 at the age of eighty-two. She made any audience feel that the best of design was obtainable, and she gave each reader the confidence to put pen to paper or shovel to dirt to give form to their dreams. She encouraged and mentored countless young horticulturalists and designers; she excelled in both, and had a great eye for color. We were fortunate to know her as a friend and to visit her home and gardens, Barnsley House, several times. We spent part of our honeymoon there and made squash soup together.

The Vereys had acquired the lovely Queen Anne stone house (a seventeenth-century rectory) and grounds in the early 1960s. In *The Making of a Garden* (published in 1995), she tells the story of how she slowly designed each part of the landscape as a work in progress, incorporating what was there while making it entirely her own. It was the beginning of her career in garden design—which started rather late in life. From her we learned many intangibles.

ABOVE: Sir Roy Strong's Rose Garden and John Taylor Monument are brilliant illustration of art elements, design principles and personality infused with personal meaning.

RIGHT: The bright blue gate at Sissinghurst is a dominant feature in the landscape and indicates the "portal."

We shared a love of historic gardens but more importantly, curiosity about the people who created them and what propelled them to manifest their dreams in this way.

From a design standpoint, we saw how to combine colors better in a perennial sweep; to give form to the ground plane with evergreens; how to manipulate space and create remarkable visual illusions; and how to stretch the limits of a potager. Barnsley's famous "Laburnum Walk" is the essence of color, scale, form and line: an art element masterpiece.

BUSCOT PARK (OXFORDSHIRE) AND IFORD MANOR (WILTSHIRE)

Both of these sites are associated with Sir Harold Peto. Buscot Park is one of his masterpieces; Iford Manor was his own home. If anyone's work influenced us with timelessness and style in landscape architecture, it was certainly his. Peto was an architect by training and loved to incorporate fragments from forgotten places. His work excels in the powerful sense of its genius loci and the use of retaining walls and beautiful steps and garden rooms with columns and chains as dividers. He made gardens within gardens.

Iford Manor has pulled us back many times. Its location on a river's edge on a steep hillside is infused with theater. Every niche is a surprise of tasteful execution and scale and is steeped with historic undertones.

Visiting the garden at Buscot Park is a unique experience and creates a tremendous sense of adventure and expectation as it pulls you along a series of water cascades and garden rooms off to the side. Along with this is an upper terrace with a

FACING: Buscot's garden rooms feature long axial views intersected by cross-axial nodes, such as this view of the rose garden.

BELOW: These steps at Iford are colored by blue campanula in natural planting pockets, softening the impact of the stone steps.

RIGHT: At Villandry, the formal parterre outside the Chateau features topiary forms and clipped pinwheel boxwoods.

BELOW: Villa Gamberaia's guard dogs overlook a panoramic view of Florence, Italy.

circular amphitheater, all quietly elegant in its urn plantings on balustrades. The water canal at Buscot is the longest we have seen; it is divided into several rooms as it flows with infinite character into the lake beyond.

France. Unlike Italianate gardens that so often transport your view to the surrounding countryside, classic French gardens are sited on vast expanses of land and are designed with bosquets of trees, walls and tall hedges masking anything that would intrude on their own highly refined sense of order and control. Vistas take your eye to a distant horizon with nothing beyond but sky. It's as if you'd fall off the edge of the earth if you ever reached that point.

The elements most relevant to contemporary landscapes are probably the confident sense of structure and the clarity of the concept. French gardens are astonishing to visit in the winter just to marvel at their bare bones. Their clipped evergreen forms are marvelous examples of holding the garden's design.

CHATEAU DE VAUX-LE-VICOMTE, ILLE-DE-FRANCE

Designed by Andre Le Notre, who later created the gardens at Versailles, this site demonstrates all the elements of aristocratic formal gardens of seventeenth-century France and epitomizes the linear ground form of major gardens during that period. Vaux-le-Vicomte excels as a total package. Its grand arrival sequence, which still functions today, sets the theme by virtue of the impressive parterres preceded by miles of pleached plane trees. Although massive compared to estate landscapes today, its scale and spatial relationships are so in proportion to the land that it does not seem overwhelmingly large, and specific treatments in the formal gardens can easily be adapted to much smaller contemporary sites.

CHATEAU DE VILLANDRY, THE LOIRE VALLEY

Villandry is a fascinating twentieth-century re-creation of what a castle garden in the Renaissance would have looked like. Its *jardin potager* consists of nine large compartments planted with vegetables and flowers in flamboyant geometric patterns.

Its most famous combination is roses and cabbages. The garden art at Villandry was a great influence on Rosemary Verey's *potager*. We love the pumpkins for autumn color.

Italy. The typical Italian garden is not about color or plants. It's about dramatic changes in level, shape and structure, airy spaces, the presence of water, statuary, architecture, proportion and soaring vistas to distant hilly environs. Historic Italian gardens blur the distinction between inside and out, with arcaded loggias that serve as roofed but open-air extensions of the house. The ways in which these landscapes invite people to enjoy nature and still feel connected to the house has much in common with the perimeter in our Four-Part Master Plan and the way people live today.

VILLA GAMBERAIA, SETTIGNANO, NEAR FIRENZE

Villa Gamberaia, considered one of the most perfect Italian gardens in existence, is very near Florence and will give you a refreshing and calm day compared to the frenzy of the city. This is exactly why noble Italian families built their villas in the countryside: to get away from it all. They made them visions of paradise—mainly by the seductive use of water. The Capponi family finished this exquisite complex of gardens surrounding their seventeenth-century Tuscan villa in the early eighteenth century. This is an excellent example of what can be achieved in 300 feet of length subdivided into garden rooms with a stunning framed view of Florence, as seen through the clipped yew backdrop.

VILLA LANTE, BAGNAIA, LAZIO

Villa Lante is known as a shining example of the Mannerist phase of the Italian Renaissance, when artists and designers were captivated by principles of proportion. Geometric forms such as the square and circle are used to great effect, and it is said that they are references to even older sites, such as the Belvedere at the Vatican and Hadrian's Villa. Unlike most Renaissance gardens, it retains much of its original structure, which is based on several terraces gradually ascending up the hillside. This site expresses a sense of exuberance, which is something we value greatly and love to impart when appropriate to the site.

Other outstanding landscape designs in Italy are too numerous to relate. However, a few others, notably Giardino Giusti in Verona, Valzanbigio in Barbarigo and Isola Bella in Lago Maggiore are candidates for the A list.

Giardino Giusti is best reached on foot through Verona's classic narrow streets. Entry through the main gate is into a large enclosed courtyard with a view into a fifteenth-century gate screen. A wide path greets you, and Italian cypresses tower above, directing your eye to the grotto mask far above on the hillside. We've been several times to drink in its magnificence and its long-reaching view over Verona.

Valzanbigio is an unusual property with a rabbitery, long axial views and beautifully proportioned fountains.

Isola Bella is an eight-acre island situated in the waters of Lago Maggiore. Along with decorative peafowl, it offers a grotto and a magnificent backdrop of masonry confections as only the Italians can create.

Portugal. Visiting historic gardens in Portugal was a revelation. We came home overflowing with ideas and were able to implement many of them in projects that followed. What stands out in historic Portuguese gardens is the lavish use of *azulejos,* the polychrome tiles that cover the surfaces of walls, grottoes, small buildings, fountains and bridges. Azulejos provide

ABOVE: The formal courtyard at Palácio de Fronteira is walled by *azulejos*–the blue in the background.

RIGHT: Loutrell Briggs, who designed this garden in Charleston, South Carolina, provides a focal point in the walled courtyard using an eighteenth-century astrolabe.

permanent color to the landscape and paint lavish pictures that tell whimsical stories. The gardens in Portugal are scaled to be lived in on a daily basis as outdoor rooms, and they make living there a joy.

PALÁCIO DE FRONTEIRA, LARGO DE SAO DOMINGOS DE BENFICA

Created in the 1660s, this garden is a great place to see and enjoy azulejos. The walls of blue tiles tell stories of multiple generations. This is a landscape narrative of the highest degree. It has year-round color exhibited in azulejos and each space seems to have its own elegant personality. Palacio de Fronteira showed us a beautiful perimeter of tightly wrapped spaces that were highly decorated: everything from chapel and seat walls to fountains. This site presented highly decorated surfaces that tell a story about the family that inhabits the site.

PALÁCIO NACIONAL DE QUELUZ, QUELUZ

This royal garden was created in the mid-eighteenth century for lighthearted festivities and sparkling evening entertainment. It perfectly conveys the spirit of Portuguese garden design—which, we believe, is not well enough known or sufficiently appreciated in the United States. The highly colored ceramic urns at Queluz (pronounced KAY-LUCH) near Lisbon give life and animate a garden during a gray, dull day in winter. This was our inspiration for the use of polychrome urns in our California gardens. Queluz is a large palace and the grounds struggle to be intimate; it is the tiles that achieve it.

The United States. Of the dozens of monumental sites in America, several have deeply personal meaning for us, beginning with the historic gardens of Charleston, South Carolina, which present gardens as a livable art form.

GARDENS OF HISTORIC CHARLESTON

To craft elegant outdoor spaces in dark and cramped places is a forte born of mastery of the craft of garden making. James R. Cothran's superb book, *The Gardens of Historic Charleston,* states: "Charleston's garden style, as it is known today, was greatly influenced by the eminent landscape architect Loutrel W. Briggs (1893–1977). Through his versatile talents as a designer, writer and garden historian, Briggs played an important and significant role in refining Charleston's garden style and in preserving and documenting Charleston's garden history."

Due to our design studio's early location in Charleston, we were privileged to restore and layer new uses on several of Loutrel Briggs' original garden designs. In Mr. Briggs' case, many examples of his work exist on paper, but only a handful of the actual gardens remain intact today.

The scale and proportion of these small gardens appealed to us in their balance and rhythm, clipped hedges and round boxwoods.

FILOLI, WOODSIDE, CALIFORNIA

Clearly one of the greatest landscapes in the United States, Filoli has classical European principles played across a coastal California canvas with views of the mountains. This place displays horticultural excellence, surprising connoisseurship in garden design in both garden rooms in the total master plan, intimate places, strong axial and vista development, close relationship to sense of place, unforgettable elegance and grace.

MOUNT VERNON AND MONTICELLO

The houses and farms of presidents Washington and Jefferson are living museums of garden history. Mount Vernon influenced our use of balanced garden rooms and high horticultural crafts. Monticello taught us about the genius of placing the house, perfectly scaled, as the hub of the property with outward-looking views.

Dumbarton Oaks, in Washington, D.C., stands in our estimation as a fully expressed, grand-scale garden on a challenging topography skillfully made into useable terraces.

Landscape movements shape our image of what gardens mean and how they functioned over time. By studying the art elements and principles of garden design, the stylistic design of great properties will unfold. It is a treasure hunt designed to hone your design skills.

This water garden in South Carolina is adjacent to the Huspa Creek, which inspired the form of the lake.

Genius Loci: The Spirit of Place

"In garden design the cardinal rule is to consider the obvious first."

—Hugh Johnson, *The Principles of Gardening* (1979)

For most homeowners, the Four-Part Master Plan has a calming effect. People recognize that it simplifies a complex creative process. Armed with logical, conceptual tools, you can analyze your own situation step by step. Instead of vaguely thinking, "I don't like the front of the house," you might end up saying something like, "I need a more coherent and inviting arrival sequence to the front door."

However, there is an aspect of the Four-Part Master Plan that will ask you, at times, to seek inspiration in another way—in the slightly more elusive world of the senses. This is the world of *genius loci*, Latin for "spirit of place." Understanding the genius loci of your property

will guide you through countless design decisions in each part of the planning process. It's the touchstone for every project that seeks to add beauty and functionality to a residential site.

The phrase "spirit of place" is frequently used by travel writers, urban designers, architects, landscape architects and garden designers—in short, those who are intimately involved with creating or interpreting sites. Its meaning often depends on context. In respect to the Four-Part Master Plan, we tend to think of it in two slightly different ways. The first is descriptive; the second is diagnostic. Depending upon how you look at it, the genius loci of a property can be either a starting point or a final destination.

To build, to plant, whatever you intend,

To rear the column, or the arch to bend,

To swell the terrace, or to sink the grot;

In all, let Nature never be forgot . . .

Consult the genius of the place in all . . .

—*Alexander Pope*

Since the concept of genius loci is so important, it is worth reviewing the first time it makes a major appearance in the literature of landscape design. The place is eighteenth-century England and the author is its celebrated poet, classical scholar and accomplished gardener Alexander Pope.

Pope was precocious, talented and, like all good eighteenth-century intellectuals, opinionated. From his mid-twenties onward, he was critical of the formal gardening style imported from France and Italy that was

fashionable among the landed gentry in England. He bristled at large gardens based entirely on symmetry and axial design and overuse of topiary. He thoroughly disliked new gardens that were arbitrarily imposed on a site for the sake of fashion. Instead, he favored an approach to garden design that seemed more sympathetic to the character of the English countryside, that engaged the viewer's eye with gentle surprises, that relied on variety and that, overall, seemed to flow from the inherent qualities of a place.

In 1731, he summed up his position in a satirical poem, *An Epistle to Lord Burlington;* it contains the much-quoted lines:

"To build, to plant, whatever you intend,
To rear the column, or the arch to bend,
To swell the terrace, or to sink the grot;
In all, let Nature never be forgot . . .
Consult the genius of the place in all . . ."

Pope was also a classical scholar. He knew that in ancient Rome, the word *genius* meant a guardian spirit; a person, family, city or institution had its own resident genius look-ing after things. In a magical sense, he is saying that every piece of land has an abiding presence available for consultation and inspiration. This presence transcends fashion and style. It knows what is right for a property and what would be wrong. "In all, let Nature never be forgot. . . . Consult the genius of the place in all." Going along with Alexander Pope, carefully study your property and understand what you have. Try not to impose too many ideas on it before you've tuned into what nature and history have already put there.

LEFT: This Atlanta garden features the Cathedral of St. Phillip as a backdrop, an unusual example of respecting the genius loci of the place.

How to Determine Your Genius Loci: A Checklist

Study the site as a creation of Mother Nature. Observe the lay of the land and the local topography. What kinds of plant materials already grow on the site and do well? What natural features are prominent—a creek, lake, marsh, pasture or views? Look at the raw materials and color palettes that are naturally there. What types of rock, stone and earth abound? What about wildlife, subtle sounds and smells? Observe the quality of sunlight that creates an envelope of sensations.

What is the architectural style and scale of the house? What are the building materials used? What are the house color palette, forms and textures?

Study the character and atmosphere of the neighborhood and its vernacular building styles. Is the neighborhood wooded? Hilly? Open and sunny? Are the houses classic or modern? Are the streets straight or winding? The neighborhood land forms, its history and how it interfaces with the larger geographic area all need to be considered.

As a descriptive term, "spirit of place" is used to capture the essence of an established property (new or old) that has an unmistakable atmosphere, a palpable character that permeates the site and manifests an unforgettable presence. Sites of this caliber have been landscaped with such great sensitivity and artistry that they leave an indelible impression on anyone who visits them. A strong spirit of place can be found on a hundred-acre estate or in a small, walled courtyard. Wherever it is, one senses quality, identity and timelessness. All of the elements seen and felt, built and planted, are in harmony with one another and with the natural site. When you are on a property like this, you have a powerful feeling of being someplace special.

The unique atmosphere and personality exuded by an unforgettable property is often studied and analyzed in Europe, Great Britain and the United States. The previous chapter highlighted some favorite examples. Creating a strong spirit of place should be the aim of all who want a special environment surrounding their home.

The other use of genius loci considers the site as a work in progress and not the finished product. It focuses attention on a process for understanding a property and knowing what will be appropriate or inappropriate when selecting materials and specific design treatments. In this frame of reference, the genius loci becomes the underpinning of the design process.

What needs to be consulted when you begin to conceive a master plan?

Listening to the genius of the place is about studying the site as a creation of Mother Nature. It includes observing the lay of the land and local topography; the kinds of plant materials that already grow on the

site and do well locally; the natural features that are prominent (e.g., a creek, lake, marsh, pasture or views); the raw materials and color palettes that are naturally there, such as types of rock, stone and earth; the wildlife; and the subtle sounds, smells and fleeting quality of sunlight that create an envelope of sensations.

It means a strong sensitivity to the architectural style and scale of the house, the building materials used, and the house's color palette, forms and textures.

The character and atmosphere of the neighborhood and its vernacular building styles are as important as the house's architecture. Sometimes, it's even more important than the architecture of the house itself. The neighborhood's land forms, its history and how it interfaces with the larger geographic area all need to be studied.

The design of the Chinese Scholar's Garden captured and re-created the spirit of place by using a five-element approach of fire, earth, metal, water and wood to represent the process of nature. They include yin/yang, hot/cold, wet/dry and dark/light. *Landscapes of Spirit: Creating a Contemplative Garden,* by Martin Mosko and Alxe Noden (2005), offers a contemporary approach to genius loci by dividing a site into air, water, fire, earth and wood.

In recent generations, the haste of land development, the proliferation of subdivisions, urban sprawl and rapid change have all too often left the voice of the muse far behind. However, no matter what you start with, it is always possible to create a powerful sense of place on almost any property by developing a materials palette that is stimulated by the house and that brings the native materials of the land into play as a design

element to create a coherent whole. The goal is cohesion in feeling and flavor.

"Consult the genius loci" is a familiar refrain throughout the following chapters. The Four-Part Master Plan rests on its venerable shoulders. The natural and man-made features that make up a property's basic character provide the starting point and creative inspiration at each phase of the process. When it comes to the point of choosing the materials and styles for new design treatments, they are the obvious reference. Staying in tune with the genius loci is what builds continuity and identity on a site.

ABOVE: The Chinese Scholar's Garden in Vancouver, British Columbia, is constructed of rock imported from China and assembled using traditional methods.

Case Study: The Benjamin Phillips House, Charleston, South Carolina.

The Benjamin Phillips House, built in 1818, provides an example of creating Hub identity and genius loci for a site that, because of time and urban development, had lost most of its original, historic context. Over the course of time, the house was subdivided into three condominiums. Its original nineteenth-century garden had long since vanished.

The design project started with a barren, concrete parking lot surrounded by chain-link fencing. However, the new owners, who are connoisseurs with a love of history and gardening, believed that the fragile voice of its spirit could be found and the site reclaimed. The well-preserved nature of the neighborhood—Charleston's historic district—enhanced this historic restoration.

The approach to the house is along a narrow, one-way street deep in the city's historic district. Its former bleak exterior presence was enhanced with the addition of street trees, roses and greenery garnishing

FACING: The brick garden structures are modeled on Charleston garden privies of the eighteenth and nineteenth centuries.

FAR LEFT: The view of the formal garden shows its relationship to the perimeter dining area adjacent to the eighteenth-century kitchen house.

LEFT: Scale and proportion were carefully studied prior to building the formal garden.

LEFT BELOW: The long façade of the house with its new gate complements the streetscape of this historic lane.

the street lamps. The property is double gated: a formal one at the street and a moon gate at the garden entry. The gates meet the stringent criteria of both the Historic Charleston Foundation and the City of Charleston's Board of Architectural Review. Roses on the main gate are *Rosa* 'Belinda' and *R.* 'Cecil Brunner' mixed with flowering jasmine, *Trachelospermum floridanum* 'Madison.'

The arrival sequence into the garden is along a deeply shaded Old Charleston brick drive that terminates at the moon gate. This barrel-arched arbor with its twin gates is cov-ered in Madison double-flowering jasmine. The Connecticut brownstone paving the threshold was found under the house in the basement and reset.

A small fountain enlivens the perimeter space designed for entertaining and provides a glimpsed view into the formal garden. Walls made of handmade antique bricks replaced the chain-link fence. Raised beds containing historically appropriate plants and heirloom camellias are arranged in a pattern of four beds typical of the period. This pattern is the most consistently used garden pattern known to man and occurs on many eighteenth-century plats. Sand-shell paths, made from reclaimed dredge material from the nearby Cooper River, bisect planting beds containing new twenty-foot trees planted for shade and privacy.

The garden received a National Award of Merit from the American Society of Landscape Architects. The judges gave it the following commendation: ". . . excellent in the cultural tradition of both city and region . . . It is confident, modest and well put-together. The garden is understated as only people working intuitively within a tradition can perform. It is superbly made."

part two

The Approach and Arrival Sequence

In Atlanta, Georgia, the
former parking area was
a large free-form asphalt
pad. The existing gazebo
became the focal point
for the new parking area,
and bluestone pierced by
an ophiopogon running
strip provides welcome
green relief.

Dignity and Expectation

THE COMPONENTS OF A FULLY EXPRESSED LANDSCAPE

The Approach and Arrival sequence is first of the four components of a fully expressed landscape. It begins at the street and ends at the front door and includes three parts: the drive portal and drive corridor, the parking court and the entry node. This part of the master plan sets the stage for an unforgettable property. Your property has a unique personality, and you can design it to create a lasting impression.

Whether located in the city, suburbs or countryside, the approach and arrival sequence is the welcome mat for visitors. This series of linked spaces takes visitors from the street to the front entrance of the house. The distance may vary from a few feet in urban settings to a few miles in the country.

This important entry corridor is often the most neglected part of a contemporary residential property. Many homeowners concentrate their efforts where they spend most of their time relaxing, entertaining or gardening. As a result, the driveway and parking area are anonymously paved and left to their own devices.

The portal involves the public interface between street and private drive. The parking court offers convenient and succinct parking. The entry node embraces and directs visitors to the front door.

Our forefathers knew how to layer the approach and arrival in a number of ways. For centuries, a long axial driveway leading up to the front of a building underscored the property's significance and impressed visitors with a sense of dignity and grandeur. Walls and gates were used to protect the house and make the transition onto the private realm of a property. Long, winding driveways allowed glimpses of the house through trees and built anticipation. Awe-struck heroines in nineteenth-century English novels eagerly glimpsed the great manor house where they might one day live (provided the romance at hand went well) as the carriage wheels lurched and leather seats creaked.

For new residential sites, the approach and arrival sequence is the historic province of the landscape architect, builder, owner and architect working in collaboration. How a new home is sited on a piece of land, how the land is graded and contoured and how the ribbon of the driveway will find its ultimate shape are solutions to complex creative problems. It is a luxury to work with a blank canvas, but many other residential projects reflect transformations of existing situations.

Keeping these visual and literary images in mind explains many of the features of the approach and arrival sequence designed for large rural estates and mansions today. The basic, physical ingredients are the same, and they play on the same human emotions of anticipation, expectation and the sheer pleasure of seeing a great house for the first time. Scaled down to smaller properties, a skillfully designed approach and arrival sequence has equally intriguing and unforgettable results.

The approach and arrival sequence for a house begins at the street by providing a welcome mat for visitors. In this approach, a gracious landing, four large boxwoods, a change of paving, a curving walk, a shade tree and a touch of color make for an inviting scene.

First Impressions

Each property is as individual as a fingerprint and can easily vacillate between model citizen and fugitive. When designing your approach and arrival sequence, three axioms will improve the process.

The first axiom is **Harmony in Materials**, which allows home grounds to read like a well-designed wardrobe, or "of a piece," as interior designers describe coordinated rooms. The second axiom is **Seamless Flow**, whereby all portions of the approach and arrival sequence work in concert. The third axiom is **Modulate Space**—by using plant materials to accent nodes or to solve visual problems.

Axiom #1: Harmony in Materials. Whether the
approach and arrival sequence is designed for a starter home
or a connoisseur's mansion, the subtle qualities of genius loci
express themselves and take shape through the introduction of
a materials and color palette. Echoes of these choices occur
throughout the entire master plan.

Choosing the predominant types of stone, paving materials and other construction materials is an exciting part of any design process. A vast range of options is available for every site: the house architecture, the color and texture of its building materials and architectural details and the neighborhood's personality. Personal preferences guide selections. The approach and arrival sequence

FACING: Walkway spaces are modulated by creating a gateway of plantings leading into the entry garden.

LEFT: A trip up this brown exposed aggregate driveway provides a seamless flow for the house and its grounds.

ABOVE: This driveway expresses harmony in materials by combining tumbled limestone edging with crab orchard cobblestone. The house is a pale buff color.

needs to say that you are encountering something special. Build the personality of the site with care and consistency.

Axiom #2: Seamless Flow. A well-designed approach and arrival sequence is perceived as one gracious and coherent whole, with one design element transitioning into the next. The portal, parking court, front walk, entry node and landing work in concert so there are no gaps in the flow.

Axiom #3: Modulate Space. Plantings add beauty and interest and are useful to shape spaces and solve visual problems. Crafted to reinforce the flow of movement throughout the sequence, plantings offer line, color, form and texture to a landscape canvas. Furnishings and accessories used sparingly give the arrival sequence additional grooming and personalization.

Harmony of materials, modulation of spaces and the seamless flow between the drive portal and corridor, parking court, front walk and landing in the approach and arrival sequence bind a property together into a coherent whole.

The Anatomy of an **Approach** and **Arrival Sequence: Checklist**

A ll properties are not created equal. Whatever its size, now is the opportunity to study, photograph and note how your approach and arrival sequence works. The following checklist for defining your portal, the parking court and entry node is useful. As in all design, the success lies in the details.

Drive Portal and Corridor

Do you park on the street? If so, is there a pedestrian gate and fencing for property definition?

How is this node treated to enhance the personality of your approach with regard to color, mail collection, pots, paving and plant materials? If the driveway pierces your property, is there a change of material at the apron? Do gates or piers define the entry at least 20 feet back to allow for temporary car parking on the street? What are the running surface and color of the drive? Can plantings be improved to express the unique personality of your property and set off the entry node at the street?

Parking Court

On which side of the house is the drive? Is it straight or winding? Is parking large enough for guests and your family? (A simple mapping tool to ensure if each car parks neatly is to provide a space 10' x 20' in size. Use survey flags available from a hardware store and a tape measure to outline the perfect arrangement. (Curved parking courts are difficult to arrange because a car is a rectangular shoe-box.) Does your parking court have trees to shade the paving? If the paving is all one piece and monotonous, could it be made more interesting with banding or a medallion?

The Front Walk, Entry Node and Landing

Does the walk direct visitors to the front door? Is it gently winding or a straight shot? Is it slammed against the house or part of the landscape? Are pots or a color node placed at the driveway to reinforce its importance? What is the paving type and color? If there are steps, do you have landings approximately every five to six steps to break up a feeling of steepness? How can you improve the impression of this being a very special place?

ABOVE: Pierced worn-brick walls offer privacy and ventilation for this Charleston courtyard.

ABOVE RIGHT: A Normandy-style house with front windows to the ground responds to a low planting accented with boxwoods to visually "lift" the house.

BELOW RIGHT: Why not let the entry landing at your home be a star? Play up large paved areas with a field of contrasting design.

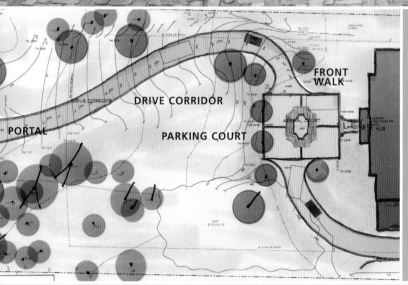

PORTAL

DRIVE CORRIDOR

PARKING COURT

FRONT WALK

ABOVE: Careful selection of rectangular slabs of gray crab orchard paving made the approach to this gem of a house less formal. Architecture by Jim Choate, Atlanta, Georgia.

LEFT: A graphic of an approach and arrival.

RIGHT: Wide steps lead to this front porch, offering room for pots to add seasonal color to the entrance and millstones for historic interest.

The drive and pedestrian gates in this Atherton, California, garden arrival sequence are covered with fig vine (*Ficus pumila*) over scored stucco columns. Lily of the Nile accents the walkway with bold color.

Memorable Moments

Approach and arrival sequence designs rely on two fundamental design concepts: the need to park your car and the size of the property. Whether you drive your car onto the property or use off-street parking dramatically shapes the design process. The size of your land, the topography, building setbacks and genius loci determine the final scenario.

The basic parts of the approach and arrival sequence are the drive portal and corridor, parking court and entry node. Linkages are routes that convey movement on a property. In this part of the master plan, this includes your driveway, path to the front door or section of sidewalk. Nodes, on the other hand, signal choices or transitions. They slow you down. Nodes include gates, steps and landings.

Understanding the personality of linkages and nodes offers invaluable insights into how the approach and arrival sequence actually functions as a combination of these two elements, flowing seamlessly from one to the next.

Memorable Moments. Memorable visual images occur at any point from the street to the front door. They are found in the marriage of two paving materials, in the charm of creeping jenny growing between the earthen joints of stepping-stones, and in the colors and paving pattern on the landing that announces the

house of a friend. Because the approach and arrival sequence often consists of large amounts of paving, a clever design requires extra imagination.

Here are some of our favorite techniques:

THE DRIVE PORTAL AND CORRIDOR

The anatomy of a drive portal and driveway corridor addresses many design elements. The drive portal includes an apron at the street, entry portal definition of the mailbox, gates and drive surface, call assist, lighting, special plants, edging, curb and gutters, plantings and entry lighting. Special considerations include the width, depth and type of the running surface, surface texture, curb selection for definition and water control, joints between segments and other construction details.

The portal, or entry node to the drive, contains four elements: the apron, mailbox, plantings and drive surface. A structured entry portal is empowered by plantings and gates to frame the narrowing view into the property. This sensation of narrowing down before progressing forward is the design principle of narrowing apertures and creates both a psychological and physical pause.

The driveway apron is the interface between the public road and your private drive. Located on public property, an apron ranges in size from 15 to 22 feet wide. The material choice for this apron literally sets the stage for your property. A change in texture, such as cobblestone paving with a slightly bumpy texture, creates a memorable transition from street to property. Your body feels the change in texture, and you hear a new sound as the tires roll over a different surface separating the street from the driveway. It's almost like fording a small stream.

The drive corridor is the drive between portal and parking court. Special attention is made to create a progression of spaces along this linkage and includes plantings, banding on the drive, curves, light and shadow.

Driveways build the story of your site. A winding drive creates expectations and a short drive is like an exclamation point. It is exciting to glimpse a house before you get the full impact up close. This builds a sense of expectation and gives presence to the hub (the house).

A driveway is usually made of a single material. If the construction budget allows for combining interesting materials, here can be an unexpected source of creativity. The addition of banding and curbing can animate a drive even if built of gravel or asphalt. The choice of curbing for drives and durability plus appropriateness to the genius loci guide selection. A curbing made from hefty weathered granite, tumbled crab orchard stone, bluestone rubble or cobblestone enhance the linear appeal of a drive.

Circular, rectangular court or straight-in are the three major choices for driveway configurations.

Examples of Drive Surfaces

There are many drive surfaces in common use. The most often used are brick, stone, concrete, exposed aggregate, asphalt, gravel and concrete pavers. The choice of drive surface depends on the length of the drive, the formality of the house, the availability of the material and your own likes and dislikes. Here are some of examples to consider.

TOP: In mountainous regions, large slabs of weathered granite provide sturdy footing for parking and, when interspersed with flat brown river gravel, allow rainfall to soak through the pervious paving.

BOTTOM: Brown and buff diamonds of concrete in two sizes bring interest to this large parking court. Limestone cobblestone banding and a central medallion visually organize the space.

FACING LEFT: A red gate and apron of stone set into pigmented concrete provide a welcome mat for this drive.

FACING RIGHT: Brown river gravel offers a crunchy sound to this driveway accented with a grass lozenge to organize the running surface.

PARKING NEATLY

The term *parking court* is applied to any driveway that brings automobiles to the front door. Think of the parking court as an entry foyer for cars. Here, you stop the car and disembark. Once your feet touch terra firma, the perspective changes to a closer inspection of the paving.

A parking court is really a parking garden. Slots for cars shaded by trees, a textured paving that interests the eye, flowers and pots all personalize this large space. One of our favorite decorative features is a central medallion laid in a contrasting paving material. A car slot is approximately 9 feet wide by 18 feet long. While in England visiting A La Ronde, we saw a sign in a pasture: "Please park neatly." Let this be a hint for the design of your parking areas.

When our design studio was in Charleston, South Carolina, we noted that about 80 percent of the historic district was paved. Islands of natural plant materials seemed to cool things down as well as help delineate spatial areas.

Paving vast amounts of Mother Nature results in the reduction of water being returned directly to the ground. Instead, water is channeled and whisked off-site into storm sewers or drainage basins. Sadly, this process contributes to the lowering of the water table and heating of the earth's surface.

Islands of grass and other plant materials offer "green relief." Green pockets and planting strips not only soften large areas of paving but also do nice things for the environment. By paving less and introducing green areas within paving materials,

A Checklist
for Your Parking

Parking Court: A Checklist

Examine the places on your property where cars are parked. Can visitors easily tell where to park and how to do so neatly? Is the area lighted? Is there room to exit a car without stepping in mud on a rainy day? Can other cars pass a parked car? Is the area inviting, an appropriate introduction to your home?

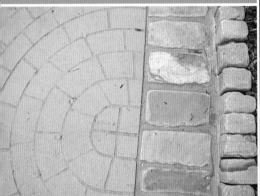

Park Here

The best parking areas say to your guests "park here" and leave no indecision about where parking should take place. Here are some examples that you might be able to adapt to your own parking area.

TOP LEFT: Scored concrete in a cobblestone pattern is edged with brown crab orchard stone for curb appeal.

TOP RIGHT: The gracious approach through woodland leads to 65' square parking court with a central medallion of granite cobbles and ophiopogon.

BOTTOM: A flat, brown river gravel separated into parking bays by tumbled beige cobblestone provides a cozy parking court.

ground water is recharged and construction materials are reduced. This makes Mother Nature happy.

THE LANDING

The landing at the front door of the house culminates the entire approach and arrival sequence. This node transitions from outside to inside and is treated with as much respect as an interior room. Here, a subtle change of paving patterns is appropriate to personalize the space.

FRONT WALK, ENTRY NODE AND LANDING

For houses with a grass lawn in front, planting beds, or both, the design of the front walk is a major ingredient for building up the genius loci. Straight walks often complement Georgian, Regency, Palladian or contemporary houses. A graceful curve is more informal and is often reserved for cottages, Tudor-style houses, and rustic properties. There are no formulas, so you simply have to let the house and the arrival court location speak to you.

Pot ears are a clever way to plan for permanent paving beneath pots that are filled with seasonal color. A typical pot ear is only 12" x 12" or 18" x 18." It gently funnels into a 5' walk at the edge of a drive.

A landing is usually associated with a few steps that lead to the house. A landing that is at least 5' x 5' square is enough to announce a front door. This entry node landing provides the opportunity to put away car keys, adjust umbrellas and rearrange a gift before ringing the doorbell. It has the added benefit of keeping you from falling into the arms of your hosts when they open the door.

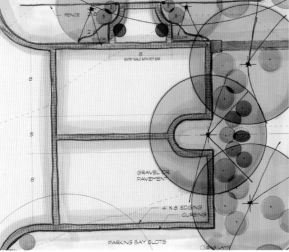

TOP: Weathered granite cobblestones are set with sedum between the joints. Bluestone trims out the exposed aggregate driveway.

ABOVE LEFT: This detail for parking with peninsula fits in a space sized 20' x 20' and parks two cars.

ABOVE RIGHT: Islands in front of the parking bays offer welcoming color, break up monotonous walkway paving, and absorb water during heavy storms.

LEED Permeable Paving

A LEED (Leadership in Energy and Environmental Design) requirement for landscapes encourages the use of permeable paving to prevent runoff of fertilizer, oil and other chemicals into the watershed and, thus, into streams and rivers. Here are some ways that this can be achieved in parking courts.

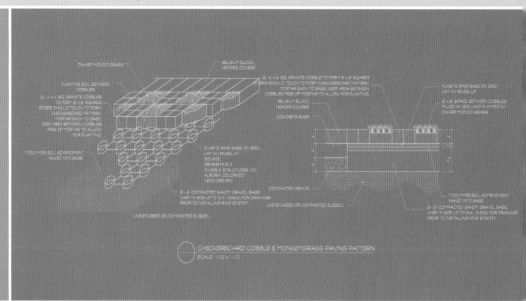

How boring this large parking court would be without zippy permeable paved areas. Grass-paved rings used for structural stability were placed beneath the granite cobblestones and topped with soil and grass.

In driveways, form follows function, so design grass or ground cover into parts that are seldom used in order to absorb runoff from the house or driveway.

A center island, or lozenge, works to facilitate water absorption in the center of a driveway.

ABOVE: Gravel is an excellent absorbant for water runoff and works well in areas of high rainfall. Architecture by Jim Meyer, Charlotte, North Carolina.

BELOW: A lay-by for guests was added to the drive opposite the driveway landing.

BOTTOM: Pot ears provide color accents and a broad, welcoming first approach.

BELOW MIDDLE: Pots and pathway plantings personalizes the front landing.

BELOW LEFT: An intermediate landing, sized 8 x10', broke up the two flights of steps.

RESIDENCE

Case Study: Approach and Arrival. The owners of this property were dissatisfied with the approach to their house. They needed a place where a car could be parked off the main drive, and wanted a more interesting arrival. Since the house was on a hill, landings were required to make climbing the stairs easier. Pot ears were placed to emphasize the front door landing. Relatively small changes made a big difference.

Creating Enhanced Walkways

Materials for Walks

Mixed materials on walkways and landings provide visual relief and add texture to large expanses of paving. Careful attention to paving patterns and edging provides a finished appearance and aids drainage.

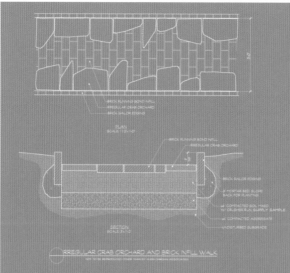

TOP: The mixed blue-stone and brick walkway pattern costs as much as herringbone brick due to the cutting involved.

ABOVE: A front walk-way through a garden features limestone slabs and ophiopogon as ground cover.

RIGHT: Three details of walks exhibit skillful masonry at corners and on running surfaces.

Design for Walks

Careful design and choice of materials for walkways are two of the things that can make a difference between a nice landscape and an outstanding one. Paths beckon us to follow and provide safe footing.

ABOVE: A detail of the "woven basket" walkway includes the bluestone banding along the lawn edge as the pathway transitions from grass to woodland.

LEFT: Large flagstones of weathered granite lead to the front of this mountain house at High Hampton in Cashiers, North Carolina, installed by John McCarley, horticulturist.

part three

The Hub

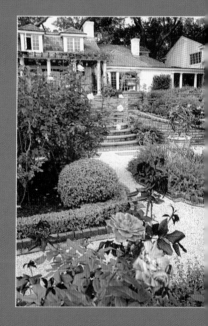

Building the Visual Connection

Greyrock Lodge, located in Highlands, North Carolina, sets an understated, mountain chic tone with stepping stones inserted in a grassy path. The entrance to "The Garden Ramble" now resembles a two-tire-track cartway.

The house, whatever its style or scale, is the natural centerpiece of a property. The second element of the Four-Part Master Plan, the hub, highlights design treatments that forge connections between the house and its site.

The hub is probably the most challenging element in the master plan and always has been. More than 150 years ago, the pioneering American landscape gardener A. J. Downing ruefully observed, "In our finest places . . . one of the most striking defects is the want of union between the house and grounds." A ride around most neighborhoods today is enough to illustrate his point. There isn't a comfortable connection between the house and the land on which it sits. The approach and arrival sequence is an integral part of the hub because it builds the visual connection of the environment with the house. The approach and arrival sequence's three

axioms of harmony in material, seamless flow and modulation of plantings produce a rhythm and cohesiveness that reinforce the importance of the hub.

How do you create the right union between your house and its setting? The house should wear its grounds like a glove and vice versa. To create a perfect fit, the process of design addresses two major considerations: 1) hub identity and architectural composure and 2) vistas and captured views.

The House as a Powerful Hub

The goal of designing the house as a powerful hub is to create a vivid presence for the house that can be grasped in an instant. This presence begins with the approach and arrival sequence and is crystallized with the first close-up view of the house. In an instant you know whether or not the house fits comfortably into its grounds.

The first design consideration involves hub identity and architectural composure. This process addresses the environment and topography of the site (its genius loci), plus the architectural style, size and mass of the house. Hub identity relates to the sensitive siting, or placement, of the house. It acknowledges that built features are part of a natural environment far larger than itself. This process affects land-use patterns, visual balance and architectural style due to the genius loci of the site. The mass, or size, of the house—its "architectural composure"—reinforces the style and

sense of intimacy or grandeur on the site. The four main categories of house massing and sizes include the mansion, mini-mansion, little architectural gem and cottage. Each of these offers unique design challenges.

Today, homes are often planned on environmentally and aesthetically challenging sites due to the trend toward denser development and lack of suitable land. Most site plans quickly encounter environmental challenges. Changes in topography can affect both use patterns and visual balance, which results in the addition of retaining walls to level the land or balance a view of a house.

The Anatomy of a Hub: A Checklist

Your property, whether small or large, includes considerations of hub identity and architectural composure, vista and captured views. Make time to study, photograph and note the way your house is visually perceived. The following checklist is useful:

- Hub identity: Is the hub approached from the side or straight on? The straight-on approach is often more formal but presents challenges if the land is not level.
- Is the ground level across the front of the building or does it slope to the side? Sloping land requires retaining walls to make a flat area along the base of the house so that plantings don't angle downhill, showing more and more of the foundation.
- Does high or low ground around the house cause drainage problems? Builders are aware of drainage problems, but the solutions aren't always aesthetically pleasing. The placement of a large catch basin in the center of a parking court as a belly button is a case in point.

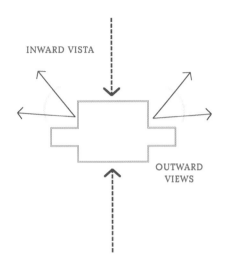

INWARD VISTA

OUTWARD VIEWS

A hub, such as a mini-mansion with its wide footprint, requires flat land for access to the garage and to reduce steps into the house from the parking areas. This configuration often results in tall retaining walls at the top and bottom of the property to create a platform, or bench, for the house to sit on. A sensitive siting of a house that requires a bench considers terracing in order to allow the house to "ride" the slope with a series of interior steps. Massing of the house is accomplished in a series of small boxes instead of one big building box.

The second consideration is architectural composure. This axiom acknowledges the style and mass, or size, of your house. There are few pure architectural styles, and a good architect will show you tantalizing examples. Italian Renaissance, Georgian, Palladian, Greek Revival, Charleston Single House, Louisiana Raised Cottage, Arts and Crafts Bungalow, English Tudor, Moorish and Mediterranean are but a few historic styles of architecture. Each is associated with a country or region that may be wholly foreign to the neighborhood for which it is planned.

What is your architectural style? Each style has building materials that associate with it and provide a springboard for landscape design. Brick, fieldstone, limestone, stucco, combinations of stucco and brick, wood and stucco and others are part of the vocabulary of your landscape design connoisseurship. Use these materials to harmonize freestanding walls and paved areas with the house.

In addition to style and materials, there are size considerations when working with architecture. Landscape design takes into consideration the scale of the house when planning terraces,

Architectural Composure: A Checklist

What is the architectural style of your house?
What is the dominant color of the building materials?
Which of these four main categories of house massing and sizes applies to your home?

▪ Cottage or Bungalow	1,000–2,000 square feet	1 story
▪ Little Architectural Gem	2,000–3,500 square feet	1–1½ stories
▪ Mini-Mansion	3,500–7,000 square feet	1½–2 stories
▪ Mega-Mansion	7,000 square feet and up	2 or more stories

Architectural composure deals with the style, size and massing of your house, as well as its relationship to the ground plane.

foundation plantings, parking courts and other grounds improvements. Your house probably falls into one of these three broad categories: mansion, little architectural gem or cottage. By acknowledging the style and mass, or size, of the house, or "hub composure," you reinforce the sense of intimacy or grandeur on the site.

Historically, houses were set upon or within a paved surface. Andrea Palladio, the Italian architect of the sixteenth century, never planned for boxwoods and ivy to set off his creations; instead, they were honest, elegant, stand-alone homes placed in large, flat areas. Foundation plantings were infrequent, and paving ran right up to the edge of the house to help with drainage. In today's world of gutters, rainfall is piped off instead of being allowed to disperse at the roof edge. Thus was born foundation planting of the house, which encouraged attractive plants and materials to accent and balance the house.

Knowing how to plant and integrate a house with its setting was self-evident in the past, when architectural styles were relatively consistent in a given time and place and plant materials were limited. Today, a few ground rules help to marry the right planting schemes with the scale and style of a house. If the house is a mansion, plant large-scale shade trees and large shrubs to help bring it down in scale. For little architectural gems, look to historic house museums and old photographs to evoke authenticity. If a cottage, practically anything goes, as long as it is intimate and personal in scale.

Improving Your Hub: Problem Solving

This technique will help you preview possible designs for your approach and arrival. Begin with head-on photographs of your house taken from enough distance to see the whole structure, if possible. If that is not possible, try to take several photographs from the same distance and put them together to make a panorama.

ABOVE: A designer's eye can work magic on even a blank canvas.

TOP: An overlay of tissue on a photograph allows you the artistic freedom to design parking areas and trees that complement the architecture.

ABOVE: A photograph speaks a thousand words, and this is a blank canvas ready for physical features.

Case Study: 99-101 East Bay. The best way to grasp hub identity and composure is to see them evolve from a single site on a blank canvas. The theme of this case study is architectural style and modulation of spaces within a historic context.

The Colonel Othoniel Beall House, 99-101 East Bay, is a most important house and garden in the context of the early preservation movement in Charleston, South Carolina, Mrs. Lionel (Dorothy) Legge, with her husband, purchased the double house when the entire block was a tenanted slum. They spearheaded the restoration of this unique assemblage of buildings into today's fashionable residential area known as Rainbow Row. During the restoration in 1930, the then owners retained the inte-

FACING: The barrel-arched, groin-vaulted pavilion at 99-101 East Bay in Charleston serves as the focal point and seating area for the garden and was inspired by the arbor at Hampton Court in England.

LEFT: Raised retaining walls of handmade nineteenth-century brick, built by Lance Leader, are capped with crab orchard stone found on the site. The large mill-stone, tile mural of Portofino and the Charleston lantern were restored and relocated on the site.

Sealed with Portland cement sometime during the 1960s, it was rusted beyond repair.

After artifacts collected by Mrs. Legge were photographed and catalogued, and measured drawings of the existing garden were conducted. Today, the rewoven garden includes 90 percent of the existing plants and artifacts.

A seating pavilion formerly on the north wall of the garden was completely rotten. However, its location as the terminal focal point on the west wall of the garden offered reconstruction of a barrel-vaulted cedar seating structure of eighteenth-century design. Old roses found on the site were mixed with a variety of vines to clothe both this structure and the groin-vaulted arbor at the garden entrance. All the existing stone and bricks on the site were reused as coping for the new retaining walls in the courtyard. A vernacular pattern of old brick and fieldstone was designed for the breakfast area; the pavilion floors echo the early paving pattern of the courtyard. A fountain was added to the north wall; the Latin inscription urges the viewer to "Look, See Beauty."

The long-lost panel of grass was reinstated. Trees and shrubs sill alive on the site remained in their original positions. The ancient Confederate flowering jasmine, *Trachelospermum floridanum,* was carefully pruned, stabilized and reattached to the kitchen house wall. A timed irrigation system—featuring drip and spray mechanics—was installed to preserve the aging specimens of tea olive (*Osmanthus fragrans*) tulip magnolia (*Magnolia soulangiana*) and camellia

grity of the building as an early-eighteenth-century structure with the ground floor a traditional mixed-use area.

In Mrs. Legge's day, the garden was the site of preservation fund-raisers and a hospitable setting for Charleston visitors. As a patron of the arts, she encouraged site-specific works and the view of Rainbow Row became the future backdrop of *Porgy and Bess.* She started garden tours to benefit The Preservation Society of Charleston in the 1930s following a visit to Natchez, MS dur-

ing their Pilgrimage Tours. Her garden was famous for its fan-tailed pigeons, iron fountain and theatrical landscape arrangement.

By 1991, the garden had been in severe decline for fifteen years. The new owners, Robert and Ann Huntoon, honored Mrs. Legge's legacy by authorizing an extensive analysis of the garden to assess the condition of plant materials and the inventory of the seventy artifacts to be saved, salvaged and reused. Still on the property was the lower bowl of a three-tier cast-iron fountain.

ABOVE: The Italian pesce
fountain was hand-carved
and includes the inscription,
in Latin, to "Look, See Beauty."
A bluestone and brick tapes-
try floors the side courtyard.

FACING: Planting pockets
offer homes to *Verbena
tenuisectus,* a happy camper
in moist cracks along the
bottom of the retaining wall.
All of the existing stone was
reset, and the existing mix of
brick and stone set the mood
for the paving throughout
the site.

variety *Camellia japonica* for future generations to enjoy.

So often, a garden is lost when its
owner moves or passes away. Thanks to
preservation interests, Mrs. Legge's former
garden functions today as a beautiful private
setting with its unique genius loci embued
by Rainbow Row. It is a lasting tribute to
preservation of the fragile garden fabric of
Charleston.

ABOVE RIGHT: The 5' wide, groin arched arbor provides a linkage node into the courtyard. It is covered with an enormous Duchess de Brabant rose transplanted from an overgrown jungle on the site.

BELOW RIGHT: The eighteenth-century Rainbow Row, otherwise known as East Bay Street in Charleston, South Carolina, is striking from this private garden vista. These "yards" were entered from the street via narrow passageways and provided a location for household services, including laundry, hen houses and small vegetable gardens. Today, they are luxurious landscapes.

BELOW: The Colonel Othoniel Beall House landscape is arranged along an undulating series of garden rooms on axis with a stately, arched pavilion.

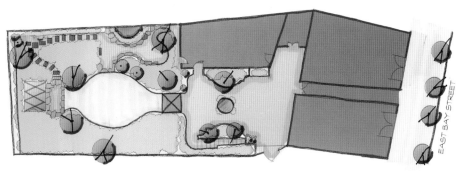

EAST BAY STREET

RIGHT: Kitchen garden features seasonal plantings.

FACING: The front entry provides a casual approach along a "void" of green. Stepping stones slow your progress and allow you to literally "smell the roses."

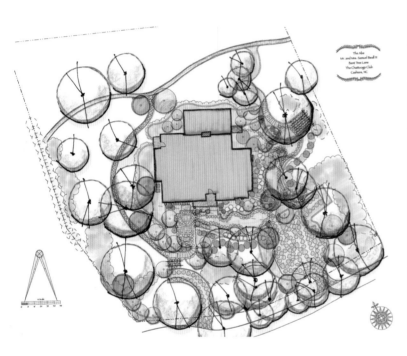

Case Study: The Abe.

A densely wooded lot in Cashiers, North Carolina, is the home of a log cabin called the Abe. The owners, who have a long-standing interest in Abraham Lincoln, seized the opportunity to re-create a period landscape for their new home from stem to stern. To blend with the house construction and imbue a spirit of place, material selections and land use patterns were chosen to be consistent with the target period of 1860–65, when Lincoln served as the sixteenth president of the United States.

This research resulted in the creation of an arrival court and short drive surfaced with native stone set into local river gravel and seeded with grass for a scruffy look. Low stone walls, reminiscent of traditional field-stone yard enclosures, announce the entry walk and are capped with weathered and slanted ashlar slabs to re-create the look of locally quarried material. Moss, sedums and ferns quickly colonized the stone cap and add a timeless quality to the entry walls. The front walk consists of irregular, local Elberton granite set on dirt and cut into a sodded lawn. This path leads to a deeply shaded porch complete with a child's rocking chair, locally made earthenware jugs, woven oak

baskets and solid log planters. Low-voltage-wired antique and reproduction miner's lamps are hung from hand-hewn black locust (*Robinia pseudoacacia)* posts.

Due to the constraints of the property size of 2.4 acres, the steep slopes and sprawling house footprint, gardens are clustered on a front and side plateau built atop an 18–22' boulder wall. Much like a pioneer outpost sited at a ledge, the retaining wall serves as a perimeter fence and is trimmed in a low retaining wall for safety.

Four gardens occur on this plateau: the Old-Fashioned Border that frames the stone path to the front door, Bud the Eagle's Kitchen Garden, the Red-Hot Mama Border

and the Vegetable Patch. Stone sets lead through the boulder wall to the garden areas in front, and a grass and locust path descend the property to connect with a network of community pathways.

Each of these garden areas has special features consistent with the vernacular approach to this unique design. For instance, Bud the Eagle's Kitchen Garden offers a mid-nineteenth-century chicken feeder made from earthenware for visiting chickens to drink water or feed. The stone-edged raised beds are outlined with rhododendron twigs laced together with burlap as plant supports. A rhododendron bench provides a place to relax. Naturalization of *Rehmannia, Chinese*

Foxglove, and *Lychnis coronaria* for summer flowers is encouraged by self-seeding in the borders. A single espaliered apple tree provides fruit. All is organically maintained. Herbs, and ground covers including *Mazus reptans* and various thymes, grow between the stones.

The Abe looks and feels old. It is not a pastiche of Americana. Instead, the Abe's setting honors the memory and methods of pioneer life by providing land-use patterns consistent with the period. The unique spirit of place allows the owners to explore their personal pioneer spirit and be in touch with their American heritage.

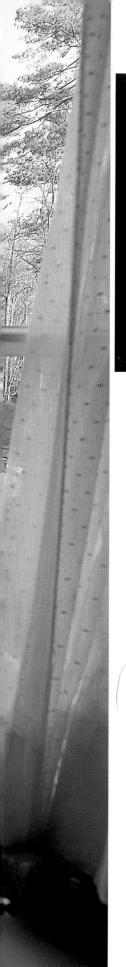

Vistas and Captured Views

Creating and improving vistas and captured views is the second design consideration.
Vistas work both ways—from the house to grounds and from grounds to house.

D one well, this design consideration fully expresses the presence of a house and is a very sophisticated and achievable treatment. Vistas are scenic or panoramic views seen through a long, narrow opening between trees or buildings. Views are particularly pleasing or composed scenes seen from a particular place. Captured views are created from windows and doors with focal-point gardens, or "eye catchers," from the inside of the house looking out to build visual links between interior rooms and the outdoors. Windows and doors are framing devices. Keep this

dynamic inside/outside relationship in mind and you will endow the hub with its unique identity.

When developing the master plan for a site, build in vistas to craft strong interconnections between the house and its immediate surroundings. A vista is a structured view into the distance, usually punctuated by a strategi-cally placed stopping point—called a focal point, or eye catcher. The most memorable vistas are constructed to have impact in both directions: outward and away from the house and back toward the house from a distant point on the grounds. Examine your property. Is there a

Axial Vistas

I n the United States, long axial vistas empowered historic southern plantation houses by focusing the view on the house at the end of a long allée.

In contemporary
America, the same
effect can be cre-
ated by careful
placement of spec-
imen trees with a
shorter sight dis-
tance. The vista to
the woodland
drive is offered
from the house
and framed by
Zumi crabapples.

When approach-
ing a house from a
long drive through
a woodland, a
framed vista across
a circular lawn
reinforces the
house as the ulti-
mate destination.

vista *to* the front, side or back of the property
that can be improved to reinforce the presence of your house? Can a vista *from* your
house be shaped?

The formal approach is based on axial
design: a crisp, clear line originates at a point
and terminates at another point in the distance. Examples include straight, paved
pathways that pull the eye directly to a point
in the distance—perhaps a fountain or
major piece of sculpture.

The great French landscape designers,
such as Andre Le Notre, created brilliant vistas
in the seventeenth century using axial design.
When creating the gardens at Versailles,
Andre Le Notre used long, arrow-straight
paths that stretched from the palace into the
expanse of the great spaces beyond; and
from beyond, he created majestic views back
to the palace. The central axis emanated from
the window of Louis XIV's royal bed chamber,
thus using the vistas into the horizon to
underscore the king's limitless power as ruler
of the land.

In today's smaller properties, an axial line
to a focal point is a useful organizational tool.
A fountain placed in line with a door opening
or a specimen tree at the end of a parking
court offers balance to a design.

History also shows us that powerful
vistas don't have to be structured by built

pathways. You can create vistas through less linear design techniques that transport the eye to a single stopping point in the distance; for example, over a grass lawn and toward an eye-catching stopping point such as a summer pavilion, a majestic hemlock tree or a pair of rustic gates.

In eighteenth-century English landscape gardens, such as Stourhead, vistas abound in a free-flowing landscape park. A structured view into the distance can float over low, rolling hills and finally be brought to a stop at a perfectly placed group of mature trees or picturesque Roman temple that punctuates the view.

Outward vistas that soar into the distance and terminate at an eye-catcher that's well beyond the owner's property line subconsciously suggests to the viewer that the grounds go on even farther than they actually do. It's a little sneaky, but perfectly allowed! Using strong vistas on large properties creates an aura of grandeur. Even without having a large property, it is possible to create scaled-down versions that still have enormous magnetism.

Captured views are created from windows and doors with focal-point gardens from the inside of the house looking out. You can build visual links between interior rooms

and views of the outdoors by using windows and doors as framing devices. Keep this dynamic inside/outside relationship in mind to endow the hub with a true sense of its unique identity.

Captured views are compositions of the outside world framed by the house's interior windows and doors. Sometimes they can be vistas into the distance that carry the eye away from the house. In many cases, they capture something just a few feet away. The idea is that what is outside has been designed and crafted to be seen in a certain way from a certain place within the house. It's as if the window or door is a canvas, and

RIGHT: The undulating garden beds narrow the focus toward this garden pavilion in Augusta, Georgia, and increase the perspective distance, making the garden look longer.

FACING: A small courtyard only 11' deep terminates the view through the dining room of the house with a stately urn 5' tall.

the view it frames is as carefully composed as a painting in which nothing could be added or taken away.

Captured views can be very simply done. So, it's always surprising that even in otherwise well-designed houses, outward views from main rooms fail to create relationships between the interior and the exterior design elements. The creative process for this design treatment emerges in different ways. It can take shape from inside the house with the simple act of looking out of a window and imagining possibilities, or it can be drawn on a master plan as a series of axial relationships that align with a specific window or door. In the best of situations, captured views evolve through sensitive collaboration with the owner, architect, landscape architect and interior designer working on the project.

In Charleston, we searched for ways to make gardens interesting and not repetitious. Every window or door had a potential captured view. A center line didn't have to be a pathway; a bilaterally symmetrical space functions in the same way. By placing a focal point at the end of a balanced, undulating set of beds, balance was achieved. This creates a vista into the distance even if the space involved is relatively short. The curves provide the shape of flower borders that flow toward the focal point in symmetrical rhythms.

Framing the View: Breaking Out of the Box. For a captured view to connect with the interior of a house, consider the interior design and harmonize the exterior view with interior colors. Chair cushions, flower borders, pavilion design, paving materials and foliage all contribute to a powerful captured view.

Vistas and Captured Views: A Checklist

If your property doesn't have beautiful views, you can design views that catch the eye and provide interest from inside and outside the house.

- Go to your property edge or to the street. Can the vista (long view) to the front, side or back of the property be improved to reinforce the presence of your house?

- Look out from the windows of your major rooms. Can you frame a vista from the house by adding an object to draw your attention?

- Look at your neighbor's landscaping. Can you borrow a view?

- Are there views from the windows that can be improved or created? Do you need a flower border, a sculptural piece or a garden ornament?

- Does this require a backdrop of plant materials or a wall or fence?

- Is the land flat or does it need a low retaining wall to provide the required 11' minimum of space beyond the window or door?

- As always, take pictures. Overlay them with tracing paper and sketch your new plan. Try several options and choose what is best.

TOP: The terrace at one former garden is a great place for entertaining. The focal point of statue and backdrop offer a captured view beneath the neighbor's window.

ABOVE: This captured view of a waterfall was carefully planned for this Buckhead home in Atlanta.

FACING: Captured views result from planning the vista from the house and back again by designing arches as part of the pavilion. The floating terrace steps lead your eye toward the house and increase the sense of perspective.

Case Study: Linking the Past.

Living in a family home shaped by layers of interaction between grandparents and offspring has its quirky ways. Pathways make desired links to a swing set or playhouse. A rose garden loved by one generation becomes a grassy lawn the next and then the cycle reverses itself twenty years later.

This is what Ann and David Hicks loved and enjoyed—living with the memories of family involvement. However, their lifestyle changed when their children were grown and brought grandchildren to visit. Places to sleep came at a premium. So, when the neighboring property became available, the Hickses added it into the fold.

Ann wanted a sympathetic blending of new spaces to address functions of today's life, such as automobile access and lack of domes-

FACING: The long vista incorporates a wishing well and guitar-shaped grass panel to modulate space.

RIGHT: The English steps lead to the rose garden that embraces the arbor terrace. A garden in the classical English sense, it includes an armillary sphere and pedestal, plus a selection of roses that are often given to friends.

BELOW RIGHT: Looking out at the water across the English steps, the columns frame the focal point of the armillary sphere made in England by Crowther's.

tic help. The decision to blend the properties was complex. It required decisions about parking, simplifying entry courts and the interface of building masses. Norman Askins, a noted architect based in Atlanta, came to interpret the buildings. He skillfully transformed a former butler's pantry into a hemisphere room—a knuckle—that allowed interface between the new guest house and the primary residence through a treillage room painted watery green.

Architectural knuckles are often found in architecture; however, they are rarely identified in landscapes, where they are called "nodes." The nodes at the Hickses' were challenging.

Vistas were created to organize new spaces. Grand outward-looking views of the John's River provided inspiration for the rear of the house, and in the front, a dynamic walkway and private garden energized the arrival sequence. The spatial and visual join-

ing of these two properties involved rethinking the paving for driveway, guest house and access to lawns and the new rose garden.

Today the two houses hold hands seamlessly. The vistas line the historic riverfront to the formal rose garden, and grandchildren play on the lawn in view of the house.

part four

The Perimeter

Extensions of the Perimeter

CREATING A SEAMLESS VISIBLE FLOW

The perimeter consists of the outdoor spaces immediately adjacent to the house and within easy reach of interior rooms. Typically, you might access the perimeter from the kitchen, breakfast room, dining room, spa, library and/or living room. These user-friendly spaces invite you to step out of the house but not stray very far. Their purpose is to provide sheer enjoyment outdoors—conveniently. As extensions of the home, perimeter spaces sustain every sort of activity, from robust entertaining to retreating from the world for a precious moment or two.

Perimeters accommodate a wide spectrum of treatments. Something as simple as a grass lawn covered with a few large paving stones might be all that's needed for an understated, low-key perimeter space. However, most households can use the extra living space perimeters afford. This part of the master plan includes the creation of paved terraces, swimming pools, grill gardens or outdoor fireplaces, loggias, arbors, dining pavilions, kitchen and herb gardens and raised flower beds.

Outdoor living and recreation areas link together through paving or garden areas so that a series of perimeter spaces wrap around a substantial portion of the house. One functional area flows into the next, creating a tightly designed but flexible network of outdoor spaces accessed at different points from several interior rooms. Alternately, specific perimeter spaces are designed as self-contained rooms. The same house might have a tiny walled courtyard off a spa, small terrace off the master bedroom, and a large, gracious entertainment terrace opening off the dining room. Each is a perimeter space, but all exist in separate worlds. Perimeter spaces expand the function of the nearest adjoining room or rooms.

Multifunctional by definition, the perimeter is one of the most flexible components of the Four-Part Master Plan. Take a small terrace, for example. In the early morning, a solitary person wanders out for a moment of calm before the day begins; that afternoon, the same space provides an informal spot for a working luncheon for a small group of colleagues; in the evening, it is transformed into the candlelit stage for an elegant dinner party with friends.

Perimeter spaces are places for people. How do you use and enjoy the outdoor areas adjoining your house? You might long for a tranquil and shady place to read, share a beverage with a partner or stare mindlessly into the garden (instead of into a television) when you get home from work. Do you entertain small grandchildren with toys spread around or take a shady nap? Perhaps, envision a small swimming pool near the house where refreshment on a hot summer afternoon lies only a few feet away. Develop your wish list. Once the functions are defined, the design of a coherent perimeter begins to fall into place.

When developing the perimeter, keep these points in mind:

■ The perimeter reads as an extension of the house; it is a seamless visual flow from the house. Attention to building materials and construction details is paramount.

■ Begin with a wish list. Be sure that it covers everything you want your perimeter space to do for you at different times of the day. Be as specific as possible.

■ Take a realistic look at your parameters. This includes all limitations and practical considerations, from budget to topography to the amount of space you have to work with.

■ Keep in mind the principle of captured views. Windows reveal what is closest to the house. Give swimming pools, flower beds, fountains and terrace seating areas a chance to perform dual roles as functional spaces and as beautiful, visual compositions framed by windows and doors. Enjoy gardens from inside as well as outside the house. As much as possible, keep grills, play equipment and cars out of sight from interior rooms.

Terraces

There are many regional variations when it comes to perimeter spaces. For example, in the mountains, a few large stepping-stones set in grass and some rustic garden furniture around an outdoor grill can be all that it takes to create a much-loved outdoor living space that intrudes upon nature as little as possible.

For most properties, paving is required to enable the perimeter to deliver on its potential as an outdoor living area. How much or how little is determined by the all-important perimeter wish list developed by the people who will use it, and the equally important budget.

The most important design treatment for adding paved surface and multifunctionality to the perimeter is a terrace. The terrace, or patio, is the paved area abutting the house no matter how modest or large the space. A terrace might be elevated above the rest of the garden or flat on the ground.

Well-designed terraces conform to the unique combination of a house and its grounds. They are completely site-specific. Creating a terrace that endures the test of time requires technical expertise. If contemplating the addition of a terrace to your house, you need to be conversant with issues influencing size, shape and materials.

The terrace's intended function determines its shape. Will it surround a pool and need an area for seating or a

The Anatomy of a Perimeter

1. Perimeter spaces expand the function of the nearest adjoining room or rooms.

2. A multipurpose, or linked, perimeter consists of a series of spaces that wrap around a substantial portion of the house.

3. A perimeter functions twenty-four hours a day—for a morning beverage, a working luncheon or an elegant dinner party.

4. How do you use and enjoy the outdoor areas adjoining your house? Define the functions of your perimeter.

5. Captured views seen from windows and doors relate the hub to the perimeter. Do your views work to extend the interior of the house effectively to the outside areas?

LEFT: Looking off an upper porch or deck into the surrounding land is a great way to gain a perspective of your linked perimeter spaces.

BELOW: This multipurpose perimeter in Sea Island, Georgia, links a small, grassed pet garden with a terrace paved with beige crab orchard cobblestones. Both are separated from the lap lane pool by a 36" planting border.

pavilion? If a grill will be on the terrace, it should have a place out of the traffic flow. A retreat for reading might need a shady outdoor alcove. A terrace that includes a fountain will need a special place for that feature. In addition, the scale of a terrace corresponds to the proportions of the house. There's a relationship between the height of the house and the width of the terrace. A three-story Georgian house needs a wider terrace than a one-story ranch.

When a terrace is at ground level, our favorite design treatment is to add a bow or semicircular shape. Strict squares and rectangles are confining and impose their form on the curves of nature. With a curved edge, the terrace reaches out into the garden and into nature; it also adds functional space since many people use round dining tables. In addition, the bow shape makes a graceful curve when a grass lawn abuts its edge.

Think of a terrace as an outdoor room with a carpet of paving. The choice of paving materials is subjective and should harmonize with the architecture, predominant materials and color of the house. Textures are a huge factor. The rough surface of a stucco house is complemented by the use of smooth, square-cut stones on a terrace. A gray or pink stucco house harmonizes beautifully with limestone with a contrasting edge of stone. From a dis-

ABOVE: In the Dowden garden, an unpaved perimeter is a wonderful place for a swing where a child can be away but still see or be seen.

LEFT: The paving, planting areas and lawn fit together like a hand and glove to provide a terrace that seems large but has minimal paving.

Perimeter Functions

Perimeters, the living areas associated with the exterior of your house, work well for dining, reading, napping, sunning, cooking, swimming, playing, working alfresco, entertaining on a large or small scale and gardening. As a result, these areas are easily customized and may include an arbor, grill, pool, fountain, sculpture, pots, chairs and tables, benches, seating walls and swings.

Dimensions of **Terraces**

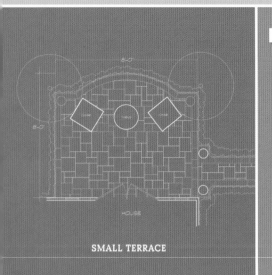

SMALL TERRACE

The Small Terrace: A cozy terrace for two includes a bistro table and two chairs with a minimum paved area of 6' x 6'. Alternately, off a dining room, a small terrace for two 48" round tables to seat four people measures 12' x 12'.

The Medium Terrace: This measures 12' x 18' and allows for versatility when entertaining. Two 60" round tables can each seat six to eight people.

The Large Terrace: An entertainment terrace of 24' x 36' comfortably accommodates three sixty-inch round tables seating eight to twelve guests each.

ABOVE RIGHT: A small terrace floored with crab orchard stone seats two comfortably.

LEFT: A medium-size terrace can serve many functions and has room for plantings as well as seating for a small group.

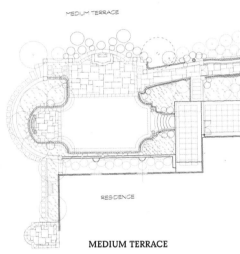

MEDIUM TERRACE

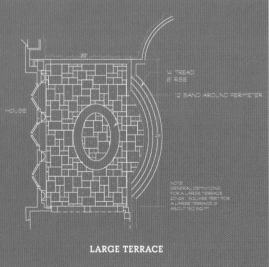

LARGE TERRACE

RIGHT: This large terrace is banded in brick with a bluestone field. Sixteen to twenty-four guests could be seated for dinner, or a stand-up party of that many could be accommodated.

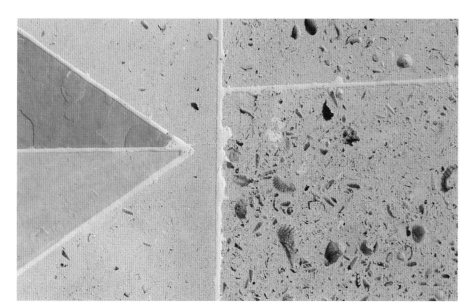

Exquisite jointing and cutting of Texas cream shell stone, New York bluestone and gray crab orchard stone.

tance, the house and terrace read as a seamless whole.

The two basic paving materials for terraces are brick and stone. The predominant stone used to cover an area such as the floor of a terrace is the "field." The edging, or "banding," that finishes off the outer edges can be of the same material or a different one. A stone field banded in brick is a typical example. Banding lends sophistication and finish. The number of possible combinations of field and banding is extensive; this selection contributes greatly to establishing the terrace's character.

Contrasts in color and texture enliven any paved area, and this is especially true of a terrace. If you want a subtle, calm and quiet effect, keep to a monochromatic palette. Don't give the impression of stopping and starting; maintain one harmonious flow.

There are countless regional varieties of materials. They can be used singularly or in combination with one another or with brick:

• Pennsylvania bluestone. It is cut in squares, rectangles and irregular shapes in large and small sizes. The hue of this stone spans a full range of blue-toned colors from green to blue to warm plumb to slate gray to

a warm brownish gray. Because of the way it's quarried, stones of the same size in a given lot tend to be the same color.

• Crab orchard stone (from the town of Crab Orchard, Tennessee). One type is a warm, peachy beige hue; it also comes in gray. When honed, this lovely stone resembles marble. Like bluestone, it is quarried in squares, rectangles and irregular shapes.

• Limestone. Compared to Pennsylvania bluestone and crab orchard stone, limestone has the palest and most homogenous hue, ranging from light gray to buff. It is quarried in squares, rectangles and custom shapes. Our favorite is Texas cream limestone, which creates a creamy, buff look. Indiana limestone, also an outstanding material, is white.

• Patina stone, made by Belgard with tumbled or chiseled edges, gives a warm look to normal manufactured brick.

• Old Charleston brick (4½" x 9") is made to look old. It is hand-cast in oversized, sand-dusted "antique reproduction" wood molds to look like original clay bricks and edges are chipped. For some older properties that are architecturally important, this is a good alternative when antique bricks cannot be found.

While there are no formulas for choosing and combining materials, consider the following:

• Brick and stucco houses respond to stone rather than brick as the predominate material on the terrace. Larger slabs of ashlar stone (square cut) honor the sleek lines of stucco. A gray or pink stucco house often looks good with a limestone field banded with beige crab orchard stone. We often add an accent note with limestone, such as a banding of crab orchard or gray cobblestone due to the high reflectivity of limestone. Even a small amount of another stone added to limestone adds depth. When limestone is used on its own, without any additional materials, it produces a very elegant, refined look.

• Wooden houses probably take the broadest range and combination of materials. Our office is a light green frame structure with every imaginable combination of materials used throughout the property. A limestone terrace is banded by tumbled granite cobbles. The front landing leads off curved steps that use a mixture of plum bluestone rectangles set next to buff crab orchard stone.

In a nutshell, the art of terrace design is to blend the materials, colors, scale and shape of the terrace with the dominant materials, colors, scale and architectural style of the house. The entire terrace composition needs to honor the contours and spirit of the landscape and natural setting. If it is done well, the terrace will simply look like it has always been there; it will just look right.

Masonry

Names of types and shapes of stones are very specific. For instance, *flagstone* is a generic term for irregularly shaped, flat pieces of stone. It is not a type of stone but a style. Far better to call a spade a spade, so here are a few terms to set you up as a knowledgeable expert.

Stone that is cut into squares or rectangular shapes is called ashlar. One of the more formal ways of using ashlar is to lay the squares in a regular pattern that looks something like tiles.

Random ashlar refers to a paving style that combines square and rectangular stones in an irregular pattern that avoids the perfectly aligned look. This leads to a more informal pattern than the squares matching edge to edge and has many applications in irregularly shaped terraces.

Similarly, brick can be laid in a variety of patterns, such as herringbone, running bond, basket weave or even pinwheels—all affecting the mood of the final outcome.

We recommend butt joints or narrow mortar joints. This shows off the stone rather than the mortar between the stones and creates a smoother surface. Also, the color of mortar, usually either buff or gray, depends on the material adjacent. Normally, we prefer to make the mortar disappear as much as possible.

Natural stones that are set as "flags," or stepping-stones, should be at least three inches thick to support the weight of foot traffic, especially when laid directly on the soil.

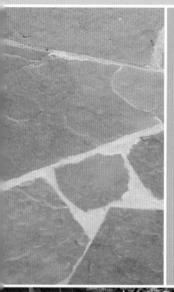

LEFT: Irregular crab orchard stone is finished with a buff mortar. Shades of buff and peachy beige were chosen to complement the warm tones of the house.

RIGHT: A brick field with irregular bluestone edging is contained by a brick sailor hedge.

FACING: Limestone set in random ashlar pattern.

ABOVE: Jumbled crab orchard cobblestones provide a sailor edge to the lawn, set with stepping stones of Pennsylvania bluestone.

RIGHT: A random ashlar, Pennsylvania bluestone terrace in variable tones with brick header banding.

The terrace vista exem-
plifies the skillful use of
outward-looking views
of the lake to extend the
site, while English steps
transition a 30" drop.
The seating bench is by
Weatherend.

Blending Functions:
Linked Perimeter Spaces

The trend in residential architecture and building is to put larger houses onto smaller pieces of land. Activities such as swimming or relaxing in a hammock, which used to take place away from the house, are now brought in closer. Multifunctional perimeter spaces are now commonplace.

Places for dining, cooking, gardening, swimming and lounging wrap around the house in one continuous picture as linked perimeter spaces. The trick to designing them is to subdivide the space with the minimum amount of obvious enclosure. Think of each specific area as a room without walls but seamlessly interconnected.

Successful rooms are achieved by a designer's sleight of hand and include several time-honored techniques. Definition of space can be achieved by a slight change in elevation between spaces, subtle texture variations, spatial dividers, enclosed or defined transitions, planting beds and the void of grass as uninterrupted open space.

Slight changes in elevation, such as raising or depressing a terrace by 12" to 18" (two or three steps) results in a conscious shift in elevation from one space to another and can take place in as little as 6' x 6'. The late Loutrel Briggs, a landscape architect in Charleston, South Carolina, in the 1940s, transformed a rectilinear series of linked spaces in private residences into a multipurpose perimeter with a vista by depressing a small panel of grass as a linkage between the dining terrace and the fountain with a single step coming and going.

ABOVE: An espalier hedge of apples makes a nice living divider to separate the upper lawn from the lower garden.

RIGHT: The treillage separates the formal lawn from the tennis court and has a very narrow footprint, enabling it to be easily inserted into a space as narrow as six inches.

Subtle changes in surface texture or the use of banding visually defines linked perimeter spaces. Brick banding is the most common. A header course is a strong 8"-wide line that outlines the edge of one paving pattern area. A band of 12" or 18" stone likewise provides a visual clue between a stone or brick terrace and grass.

Green walls of hedging or latticework provide verticality to separate one space from another. These may be as narrow as a 4" post with lattice or as wide as a 30" hedge or an 18" wall. It all depends on the parameters of the space and adjacent uses.

One of the best ways to provide visual and spatial transitions between areas is to enclose and define an entry with a gate, arbor or set of columns. A moderately sized arbor of 5' x 5' is enough to separate a terrace from a swimming pool. A gate may be executed in 4" of space and span as little as 28" inches. Again, it depends on the adjacent uses and size of the space. The use of a pair of columns or pyramidal plants is a simple visual aid to define an entry to another space.

Planting beds provide color and spatial divisions, plus the fun of gardening close to the house. Horticultural collections of herbs, geraniums, rhododendrons, Japanese maples or other plantings provide interest when placed close by the house in linked perimeter spaces. Pots at corners define spaces and can be refreshed at a moment's notice before a party. Keep in mind that many of these design treatments have the additional virtue of camouflaging unwanted views. For example, planting beds provide growth space for shrubs like sasanqua (*Camellia sasanqua*) or tea olive (*Osmanthus fragrans*) that provide year-round screens.

Because the intensity and diverse activities in multifunctional spaces can bleed from one space to the next, a small lawn may provide a rug for activities and offer visual relief. An uninterrupted plane of grass provides a void, a breathing space. Against this void a flower border, terrace or pool shows off to great advantage. In Charleston, South Carolina, a visually successful garden typically consists of a long rectilinear courtyard divided into three spaces: a terrace; a void of green; and a garden or swimming pool area. These proportions adapt well to larger spaces and provide linked perimeters that are energized with a diversity of surfaces and environments.

Dining Areas. Outdoor dining is a luxury in many climates and a seasonal necessity in others. Despite heat, sun exposure or constraint of interior space, people have migrated outside to dine for generations. It is fun to dine alfresco, but challenges abound. The amount of seating, size of terrace and amount of available flat space are key ingredients to success.

A furniture plan drawn to scale is essential for planning a dining terrace. It is a flexible tool for fully expressing your multifunctional space. Round tables are often more useful than rectangular ones. A rectangular table of 40" x 60", seating six, works well; a rectangular table seating ten or more poses a problem in communication between the two ends, resulting in a dead space in the middle. Two 60" rounds provide a better conversational environment.

A typical terrace designed for a party of six may be executed in a space sized 12' x 12'. A larger party for ten requires 12' x 18'. A cocktail party with twelve couples (twenty-four people) needs 2½ square feet per person, resulting in 600 square feet or about 20' x 30'.

Side tables and étagères are highly useful and often overlooked in planning a dining terrace. A two-tiered étagère with an 18"-

Furniture

imeless furniture begins with wood and ends with iron and aluminum. Furnishings for outdoor uses must be comfortable in all weather and not too large. Wood is the best in any season, but it takes a while to dry. We prefer Iroko wood or farmed teak. Our favorite furniture styles are elegantly scaled, classically styled pieces made of cast aluminum. Light to carry, these pieces are quite durable and will be handed down through generations. Small box pillows make them comfortable for long-term use while dining.

LEFT: The Talbot, with its tile insert, is a decorative and comfortable cast aluminum settee.

BELOW: Iroko wood furniture set on a random ashlar Crab Orchard stone terrace.

wide surface and 4' or 6' length is essential for serving and can serve as a decorative accessory between functional engagements.

Grill Gardens & Outdoor Fireplaces. Part and parcel to a dining terrace is the grill garden. Grill gardens can be highly personalized to include prep areas, the cooktop, seating and serving. Since grills vary from 24" to 48" in size and can include a side burner for boiling water, a cooktop can extend to 10' in length.

Overhead structures are often included to provide a waterproof cover for the chef. We once provided umbrellas for guests during an inopportune shower as the roasted vegetables and sausages slowly cooked in the anteroom of our tented, claret pavilion. A good tip is to place the grill near conversation-friendly areas and enjoy the company of others during the cooking process.

The outdoor fireplace is a fun and functional place in the landscape. One client asked for an outdoor fireplace with a twelve-foot opening so her Cub Scout pack could cook marshmallows close to the house. We provided a seating wall and a raised hearth for them to perch on and toast their treats. Outdoor fireplaces can morph between providing heat on a cold day and food on a hot day or can act as a

tension lifter at a stuffy party. Everyone loves to gaze into a fire.

Kitchen Gardens & Flower Gardens.

Most of us enjoy gardening in flower beds near the house and creating small gardens for veggies and herbs nestled in spaces adjacent to the house. What is nicer than picking a fragrant bunch of herbs on a slow walk around your terrace? Plan ahead and determine which beds in the perimeter have the most daylight and which plants you'd like to have in combinations near the kitchen or terrace. Raised beds can do double duty as planting beds and seating walls if they are 18" high—convenient for people with bad backs.

TOP: Fireplace detail with raised hearth.

ABOVE: Multifunctional terraces often feature an outdoor grill adjacent to the dining area. A typical 36" grill with its outrigger mechanizations for food prep, side burner plus controls occupies a minimum of 5' x 3'.

ABOVE: This pool in Sea Island, Georgia, tightly connects to the house and part of the daily use areas of linked perimeters. The amount of paving was reduced around the pool with stepping-stones set into grass, which aids informal gatherings with dogs and children.

BELOW: The vanishing edge of this swimming pool in Sea Island opens onto the marsh where storks nest. The pool interior reflects the color of the surrounding environment.

Swimming Pools. Swimming pools in multipurpose, linked perimeter spaces must be very carefully planned. Design considerations include size, color, decking type, cover type, lighting, interior surfacing, coping and the inclusion of a spa. There is no rule of thumb for swimming pools because sizes vary depending on the type of pool and whether it be a lap pool or a wider, double-laned pool of 20' or more.

Lap pools—a popular concept for small, narrow spaces—are most gratifying as art objects. Generally no more than 12' wide, they vary in length from 35' to 60'. Our favorite size is 40' because it offers most swimmers an even number of stokes.

Artistically, a narrow body of water such as a lap pool provides opportunity in a linked courtyard to be considered an art object. When placed on axis with the rear door as the focal point of a terrace, a lap pool excels in providing magnificent captured views. For example, the reflective surface of the water can magnify the outdoor space by reflecting a backdrop, surrounding trees or sky. Adding jets to create a spray on the surface or arching over the water makes for an especially refreshing picture. Also, the use of a vanishing edge on the swimming pool is a spectacular way to imply a broader vision into the distance. By visually blending the edge of the pool with the landscape beyond, this technique extends the perimeter, making a limited amount of surface area seem unlimited.

TOP: Steps from one perimeter level to another provide comfortable transitions when using compatible materials and designed as part of the whole picture.

ABOVE: This small lawn is tentable with a 20' x 20' module for parties and communicates well with service and pool areas seen in the picture above.

The Great Lawn. Large grass surfaces provide forums for tented parties, wedding receptions or garden parties. Think of a large grass lawn as an outdoor room waiting for its roof.

Plan ahead for the ultimate party by running electrical outlets and providing strategically placed water connections. Great lawns can be many shapes. We tend

LEFT: Croquet is fun, and a large, flat area is perfect for family games at this home in Florence, South Carolina.

FACING BELOW: The fig-covered steps offer a gracious transition from pool area to grassy playground in Sea Island, Georgia.

ABOVE: The great lawn at the late Phil Walden's estate in Atlanta replaced a former kidney-shaped pool. A 40' x 60' tent will fit this space.

to scale most to fit a standard tent, such as 20' x 20' or 20' x 40'. Tents of these sizes will hold three or five 60" tables, a bar and serving tables for a party of eighteen to thirty-six people.

When a great lawn adjoins a dining terrace room, be sure that the slope will carry away rainfall and still be flat enough for tables and chairs, and be mindful that the placement of future trees in the garden surrounding the lawn will not interfere with future tent place-ment. Small trees—such as Japanese maples, crab apples or other types placed within a flower border—or shrubbery should be at least 10' from the lawn area.

Furnishings. The selection and placement of furnishings and accessories plays a major role in defining perimeter spaces and suggesting traffic flow. This is where the lifestyles of the individuals using the space come into play.

Furnishing perimeter spaces needs to be done with the same care as you'd take with your living room or dining room. Attention to all the details that build ambience—especially lighting—is what gives the perimeter its ultimate sense of being an extension of the house.

This gracious, limestone-columned pavilion in Buckhead is scaled for a diminishing perspective view from the house with 8' columns.

Loggias, Arbors and Pavilions

Even in the mildest climates, people like to have a covering over their heads when enjoying an alfresco meal or simply relaxing outdoors. For centuries, loggias, arbors and pavilions have provided comforting canopies, and each can be a self-contained and highly functional perimeter space on its own.

We make subtle distinctions between garden structures that define their use. Their definitions in the literature of garden design and landscape architecture are somewhat flexible. The following describes how you might think of them.

Loggias

Loggias are steeped in history; they go back to the ancient civilizations of the Egyptians, Greeks and Romans. Originally, they were colonnaded galleries or arcades. During the Italian Renaissance, they received renewed attention in the country houses that provided a respite from the heat and noise of the city for those able to afford a villa.

In the country houses designed by Andrea Palladio, loggias were built as colonnaded extensions of an interior room. They offered a cool, airy space that provided a transition from the house's interior to the outdoors and that captured the breezes and views of the countryside beyond. Today, following the Palladian idea, in residential architecture we think of loggias as structures that project from an exterior wall of the house or that open from an interior room, or rooms, and have a solid roof supported by columns.

In houses with classical or neoclassical architecture, loggias sometimes function as long porches at ground level or higher. In southern homes, you might find loggias with large ceiling fans used to stir breezes in the summer doldrums and a few rocking chairs or wicker benches and side tables. (In Charleston, South Carolina, porches are known by the vernacular term piazzas.)

Large loggias can support a myriad of activities including full-scale dining and grilling, especially if they open off the kitchen or dining room.

Loggias are considered part of the house and are often designed by the house's architect. We consult on building materials, furnishings, climbing plants, pots and other accessories to integrate this space into the rest of the garden and site.

FACING: This classic loggia is at Iford near Bath, England. Home to noted architect Sir Harold Peto, who studied in Italy and loved all things Italianate, the loggia easily seats eight for dinner and has several benches and tables.

ABOVE: Andrea Palladio, the famed sixteenth-century Italian architect, popularized a building form consisting of arches and columns, similar to Hadrian's Villa. This pavilion extrapolates that idea in an outdoor structure. Bench by Weatherend.

Arbors

Like loggias, arbors shelter stationary activities, especially dining or relaxing. In these airy structures, vertical supports hold up horizontal rafters, creating a ceiling open to the elements. They handle an abundance of plant materials that add shade, fragrance and sensuality to any outdoor spot.

In the perimeter, we often add an arbor onto the exterior wall of a house that has a door or doors connecting to the outside. This elegant, vine-covered arbor enlarges a small house and adds instant charm and graciousness to a larger one.

Equally satisfying is the technique of adding an arbor to camouflage an unattractive building that cannot be moved. One of our favorite examples was an arbor added to a small garage in a walled garden in Charleston, South Carolina. The owner decided to have the

garage double as a space for parties. The interior of the garage doors was faux painted with murals; the concrete floor was transformed into faux stone. During parties, guests circulate through the garage's french doors and spill out into the garden and small lawn through the arbor.

Arbors 12' x 18' or 12' x 24' are great sizes for dining or seating. A paved floor is usually desirable, since grass doesn't work well with tables and chairs. The floor plane should be level with the door or doors that connect it to the house and should feel like an extension of the floor of the interior room it adjoins.

Although cedar and treated pine are excellent choices for columns, the most durable material is limestone, which works especially well in settings where other structures are

Elevations and Materials for Arbors

Common materials for the rafters of arbors include western cedar, cypress and treated pine. The posts are often made of treated pine or cedar. We often use the simple classical columns (Tuscan or Doric) as supports. They usually sit on a 2"–4"-thick square stone base. Stone is important for resisting water damage.

LEFT: During construction of this arbor, the scale of joist and beams was carefully studied.

BELOW: Made of antique cypress posts and rough-sawn cedar, this arbor extends the use of the garage behind and presents a pretty façade.

made of brick, stucco or stone. Limestone columns lend a feeling of stability; and they never need to be painted.

Fiberglass columns are also available and look almost exactly like wood once they're painted. Fiberglass columns make a hollow sound when tapped; be sure to fill with sand or foam insulation.

Architecture guides the selection of materials. For example, if the house is a Regency or Federal design, an arbor made of iron is a great choice for a light, refined look. Typically, iron arbors are dark in color, creating a dense feeling of canopy compared to wooden rafters.

In creating iron arbors, we work with an iron-smith to customize designs. Prefabricated versions are seductive, but we recommend testing the scale, because they are often under-scaled and look flimsy. In general, pre-sized structures are to be used with caution because they tend to be under-sized and out of proportion.

In warm climates, ceiling fans installed in arbors really help to stir the breezes, making dining more comfortable. Lighting strips recessed into the rafters are desirable.

For evening ambience, we suspend glass candle holders, such as colorful Venetian globes or pierced, worn tin lanterns. Also, hurricane lamps protect candle flames from breezes. In general, candlelight cannot be beat for arbors.

An arbor would be bereft without flowering vines or climbing plants to clamber up the columns and create a thick canopy. Suggestions for plant materials vary from region to region. Use dynamic trios or medleys of vines that bloom in three seasons such as *Rosa chinensis mutabilis* (butterfly rose), *Clematis armandii* (leatherleaf clematis), *Polygonum aubertii* (silver lace vine) or *Gelsemium sempervirens* (yellow jessamine).

Not to be overlooked are the shadow patterns on the ground created by the rafters covered with billowing vines. Fluttering movement on a breezy day is very conducive to happy reverie.

LEFT: The Cathcart pavilion is a roofed structure with a strong central arch and small flanking chambers for storage. The arched arbor repeats the shape of the terrace and provides a welcome visual relief from the rectangular courtyards of Charleston, South Carolina.

ABOVE: This pavilion is as beautifully made as a piece of furniture. White lathe covers the roof and gentle arches round out the front profile.

Pavilions

Pavilions evoke the glamorous history of lavish entertaining that reached its height in the gardens of the French monarchy and in royal circles in the seventeenth and eighteenth centuries. Created by the leading architects of the day, they were elegantly designed, tented structures that sheltered outdoor dining parties, concerts and festive gatherings. Sometimes they were made of fabric; other pavilions were solid structures built to last. Pavilions provided a much-needed respite from the rigid structure of court life and signaled relaxed outdoor festivities. Today, pavilions can be as ephemeral as a party tent or as permanent as a small building. Over the centuries, they have lost none of their ability to delight and amuse.

Styles are diverse, ranging from Palladian to mountain vernacular. Pavilions usually consist of a roof supported by columns. We advise that you site pavilions in destination areas or in the perimeter as dining pavilions. Pavilion tents come and go on a "great lawn" sited just a few steps away from the house. Like arches and pergolas, pavilions are wonderfully versatile structures throughout a property.

Pavilion Inspirations

The location of pavilions in the landscape is best thought through with relation to all the elements in the garden. Open rafters provide a sense of enclosure yet airiness to roof lines, making the structure less imposing in the landscape.

LEFT: The Palladian pavilion was distilled from the window shape overlooking a pool terrace and set 100' from the house.

BELOW: The pavilion is situated near the back door and is convenient for al fresco entertainment.

FACING: This Charleston courtyard is 30' and 11' wide. Retaining walls help organize space, giving the illusion of movement, and provide seating areas.

LEFT: A set of flowing steps pierces the low retaining walls and graciously transitions the 18" drop.

Sanctuaries

Even though courtyards and walled gardens are self-contained worlds, think of them as an element of the perimeter space since they are usually tightly connected to the house.

In addition to offering tranquility and solace, courtyards take pressure off the house by providing extra space for dining and entertaining outdoors. A courtyard is any small-scaled, walled enclosure that functions as an outdoor room or as a series of small, adjoining outdoor rooms.

The main qualities of a timeless courtyard are privacy, a sense of intimacy and a roomlike ambiance. Consider the following elements de rigueur for any courtyard deserving of the name.

- Walls of character
- Floors created from interesting paving
- An arbor or shady seating area
- Areas for seating and/or dining
- The cooling sound of water
- Seasonal plants and summer shade
- Comfort and style created through lighting, furnishings and accessories

Courtyard gardens come in many sizes and shapes. In tightly built quarters, such as the historic district in

Charleston, South Carolina, a courtyard often occupies the leftover spaces between two buildings. In courtyards, one or two of the four enclosing walls are provided by the exterior of house; the other walls are freestanding structures built of brick, stone or wood.

The height of enclosing walls establishes privacy and enclosure. The wall height for a courtyard is 6' to 8' and is determined by local building codes.

Materials for walls and enclosures vary from stucco walls seeded with oyster shell and capped with stone to weathered or painted wood. Pierced-work brick allows air circulation. As always, materials for construction should be chosen to harmonize with the house rather than stand alone.

Unless walls are old and weathered, they usually need softening with climbing plants and treillage. Include a 12" to 18" planting bed in front of or behind a wall to allow vines to thrive. A few strategically placed vine holes (8" x 8", or the size of two bricks) allow plants to flourish, especially if irrigation is provided.

When planting espalier plants, carefully remove the wooden frame and attach the plant to the wall surface by means of a vine eye and sinker.

Treillage softens a blank wall and provides support for climbing vines and espalier shrubs. Iron is most durable and when painted the color of the wall provides a subtle 3-D effect. Wooden lattice panels can be enlivened by arching the panel or using lathe spaced horizontally and vertically at 2" or 4" intervals. Most houses need custom

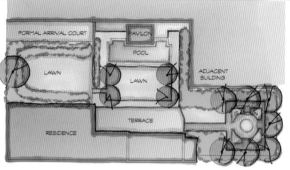

The Anatomy of a Courtyard

Courtyards are unique microcosms that occupy a small walled space. These are linked perimeters at their very best and offer a range of activities all seamlessly connected—dining, playing, entertaining, gardening, napping and interface with arrival sequences for cars and people. In addition, the tight configuration of spaces produces some very clever design solutions for hiding trash or softening a tall wall. Design styles vary, but the two most often used are the picturesque and formal.

FACING: The new wall backing this sundial has jack-arched panels, distressed stucco and a slanted brick cap.

LEFT: The garden at 58 Meeting Street in Charleston, South Carolina, was a former parking lot and is now a diminutive garden 14' wide and 30' long. To make it seem longer and wider, a picturesque approach was used for the central brick node. Low seating walls of only 12" edge the beds. The iron treillage was custom designed to add movement and support for vines.

LEFT BELOW: The bluestone flooring matches the coping of the fountain basin and provides unity in this Atlanta, Georgia, courtyard garden. The fountain adds a cooling splash.

treillage to fit the scale and proportions of the available space.

In addition to enclosing walls, courtyards have paved floors to accommodate seating and tables for outdoor functions. Materials are chosen with the same care devoted to selecting the perfect rug for the living room. Build in small planting beds and keep the use of pots and containers under strict control. Too many pots can clutter a small courtyard.

Our favorite courtyards greet visitors with the refreshing sound of water splashing

Seating in a courtyard, like everything else,

requires forethought with an eye to finishes and styles that fit the exact space for which they are intended. In courtyards too small to handle furniture, a low seating wall can be incorporated into the design.

in a fountain or murmuring in a small pond or water feature. A fountain provides a perfect focal point in a town courtyard and also buffers noises. Courtyards, especially in warm climates, can have built-in hums and buzzes from air-conditioning compressors. In town courtyards, vehicular traffic noises spilling in from the street are an unwelcome intrusion. Setting a fountain, even a small

FACING: Gray walls, gray Pennsylvania blue-stone paving and mono-chromatic seating unit colors create harmony and bring visual breadth to this tiny garden.

LEFT: A brick privy building is covered with Florida jasmine and Belinda's Rose.

ABOVE: Banksia roses frame the view of the Italian-made bas relief of a fish that reads *ubi estas sata fioretta* (bloom where you are planted).

one, within a courtyard offers a soothing sound that helps to mask outside noise and enhance the sensation of peacefulness.

A courtyard can be designed to feel more spacious than it actually is. Select a cool color palette and carry it out on all the major surfaces, including walls, floors and furnishings. Not only will this enlarge the space but it also will create a sense of tranquility. With

regard to planting beds, remember that darker tones recede into the background while lighter ones spring forward.

Designing for these inherently calm and private spaces is about character, charm and graciousness. Every detail is magnified in a courtyard, thus it is essential to have an unflagging respect for the materials, to strive for impeccable craftsmanship and to study

long and hard before choosing plants and accessories. The goal is not only to maximize the feeling of spaciousness in a relatively small area but also to create an environment that feels completely uncontrived—as though it's always been there and always will be.

Walled Gardens. In comparison to courtyards, walled gardens encompass a greater variety of sizes and shapes, and are not as narrowly defined as outdoor rooms. They enclose lawns, swimming pools, pavilions, pathways, formal flower gardens and parterres and other design treatments that articulate the space and offer more variety and functionality than the room-oriented courtyard.

In large walled gardens, with matching budgets for design and construction costs, a small courtyard might even be tucked into a larger walled space—perhaps off the master bedroom or indoor spa. Many walled gardens, such as those in Charleston, South Carolina, comprise the Four-Part Master Plan in microcosm. You experience the approach and arrival sequence, hub identity, perimeter, and passages and destinations all rolled into one highly refined, enclosed space that can be seen simply by looking over a tall picket fence from the sidewalk.

Enclosures And Walls

At our former home at 78 Society in Charleston, South Carolina, we enjoyed playing with color and designed our courtyard wall as a frame enclosure. A former Montessori School in a very urban setting, our home had a courtyard that was once a paved parking lot. Now a lovely oasis of green, it is a serene retreat and the home of a popular day spa.

FACING: This domestic wall ensemble of recycled granite logs faced with Tennessee fieldstone subordinates a 22' hillside slope by articulating surface and changing rock patterns.

ABOVE LEFT: The grotto appears to be a natural flow from the solid rock behind, but it is actually recirculated and trickles over the rocks to mimic a mountain spring. Potted ferns are sometimes tucked into small shelves in the grotto and seem to be growing there.

ABOVE RIGHT: The same garden functions well for grandchildren and community events, such as the Joy Garden Tour that benefits The Village Green in Cashiers, North Carolina. Pathways are punctuated with seating areas.

part five

Passages and Destinations

Exploration and Enjoyment

INTENSIFYING THE SPIRIT OF PLACE

The last part of the master plan is about design elements that invite exploration and enjoyment of garden environments set away from the house itself. This is where the pragmatic concerns of site planning give way to flights of fancy and pure poetry.

Passages structure movement around a site and take you to destinations—places designed to entice you away from the house for recreation or relaxation. A destination can be as simple as a weathered wooden bench under a tree or as elegant as a Palladian summer pavilion. This section looks at a range of destinations on a variety of properties from flower borders to croquet lawns to pavilions or secluded garden rooms.

Most home landscapes have between one and three destinations. Relatively few play them up to the extent they deserve. Our intention is to show how passages and destinations can be creatively conceived together to intensify the personality of a property and its spirit of place.

These crab orchard steps were cut on-site to create a round landing and circular steps that lead into a cutting garden in Charlotte, North Carolina.

Getting There

Part four of the master plan concentrates on areas of the property set at a distance from the back of the house. Passages, the walkways specifically designed for reaching these places, consist of two master connectors: linkages and nodes. In this case, pathways and walks leading away from the house to various destinations are the linkages. The intersections or moments of transition along the way are the nodes.

The first role of linkages is pragmatic: they provide logical circulation routes. Well-designed linkages effortlessly convey you around a property and gently deposit you, at the right moment, at specific destination spots. Their secondary role is to define a strongly designed ground form. In addition to getting you from point A to point B, linkages are lines whose shapes and scale create a pattern on the ground. Pathways and walks make ribbon-like imprints upon the land that form a graphic design. They have a double life: all linkages get you someplace, but they also articulate the ground plane. The impact is not only graphic but one of mood as well.

Whenever you work with line, you are working with an expressive force; you have the opportunity to create a particular feeling or undertone.

It is challenging to determine a property's circulation routes. One is always working with the site's parameters—its limitations and possibilities. If a site is essentially a large, blank canvas, it's up to the designer to create the concept. There is never a formula; it's a matter of balancing variables. Also, part of the challenge is devising functional linkages that provide a circular route around the property.

Walk around and get a feeling for the grade. Is it flat? Is it sloping? Should the grade be changed to gently flow

RIGHT: Kitchen and formal garden paths are typically 30" wide to enable access for a wheelbarrow or small cart.

FACING ABOVE LEFT: A brick walk of simple pavers interests the eye with its smooth "curve and tangent" transition at the corner.

FACING ABOVE RIGHT: A grass path in a large southern garden is lined with blue hydrangea. The pathway is 5' wide.

FACING BELOW: Limestone rectangles 18" x 24" and squares 24" x 24" enliven a formal walk planted with mazus and pratia blue star.

The Anatomy of a Path

Pathways to destinations are variable in materials and width. A rule of thumb is that for two people to walk comfortably side by side, a space of five feet is needed. If a single person is enjoying a private walk, then 24"–36" is sufficient.

up or down from a given point? What is around the edge of the site? Should a buffer of trees and shrubs be planted to form a protective visual envelope? Study the scale and shape of the piece of land you are working with. Do you need a focal point? Does the space call for a long grass area with formal lines or asymmetrical shapes?

When determining the ultimate shape of the passages on a site, function is a primary consideration and the key question is: What are the destinations that the routes lead to? For example, will there be a swimming pool? A flower garden? A shady woodland walk? A private retreat? The location of each is determined by available land, topography, tree locations and a sense of the arrival sequence. Once the destinations are established and their placement decided, move

forward with the whole process of designing the linkages.

Pathways

Pathways and walks comprise one of the most subtle but powerful aspects of the entire composition in the Four-Part Master Plan. Once people leave the confines of the perimeter, their movements are highly structured by the linkages upon which they tread. Pathways are an incomparable tool for intensifying and consolidating the genius loci. In designing them, look at lines, colors and construction materials that complement the architecture of the house, the architecture of garden destinations and the mood you want to emphasize.

For a path, consider using a long S-shaped curve; it is an almost archetypal form that has long been associated with a feeling of grace

and tranquility. In the eighteenth century, the English painter William Hogarth called this shape the "line of beauty" and argued that it added elegance to any composition.

Other curves bend and are more winding. On a large property, a meandering path and tall plant materials can be used to conceal the final destination until you are suddenly upon it. This element of surprise is more appropriate for informal landscapes or informal sections of a larger design comprised of formal and informal notes. It is the hallmark of English picturesque landscape design. This is what Henry Hoare did on his property, Stourhead, which is a masterpiece. On more modest properties, a curvilinear path takes its shape because it is affected by an immovable preexisting object, like a tree or groups of trees. Often, obstacles can be turned into

advantages. By a creek or riverside, long, elegant curves executed in gray stone can mimic the water's form.

When the house architecture and genius loci suggest a more formal approach, crisp, straight lines are often the most appropriate choice. Axial and cross-axial designs are the underpinnings for a stately ground plane when a feeling of rationality and functionality overshadows romance and whimsy.

The principle of focalization comes into play on plans that utilize straight lines. It is interesting to be walking toward a focal point on axis, or toward a view that's been accented by an arch or framing device. Similarly, why not place something special at the intersection of two straight paths? When you start thinking in these terms, your passages become much more than a way to get from point A to point

B; they start to manifest their true potentials as elements of art and design.

Working hand-in-hand with the shape of pathways and walks are the materials from which they are built. As always, materials should be chosen in accordance with the genius loci in colors and textures. Pathways offer bountiful opportunities for sophisticated paving treatments and the combination of materials such as old brick and bluestone.

Pathways should be no less than 18" wide for single file or 60" for two people side by side.

Nodes are the all-important intersections along a pathway or route where you shift gears and often come to a stop. The crossing of two paths is a node. Which way will you turn? Nodes can be played up and accented with an arch, pergola or gate. When a change of grade is involved, a node can also be graced by a set of steps.

Nodal structures add intimacy and pleasure to any garden ramble and provide strong focal points to punctuate the overall composition. Recognizing where to install points of transition throughout a property and implementing them skillfully takes a landscape design to another level of sophistication.

LEFT: Limestone-banded step ramps anchored with boxwood planters provide seating flow effortlessly down the gentle slope of this home in Belle Meade in Nashville, Tennessee. Architecture by Terry Bates.

RIGHT ABOVE: Sometimes a small elevation change of 12" to 18" can provide great interest to a garden node.

BELOW LEFT: Important to step design is attention to the landings at the top and bottom of stairs.

BELOW RIGHT: The 3' wide entry to this kitchen garden in Atlanta, Georgia, is punctuated by a pale green arch set with a Craftsman-style gate.

Arches

Traditionally, nodes have been considered perfect spots for the use of arches, and this is still true today. First of all, they serve as focal points that attract you along a route and provide a sense of expectation or anticipation. Due to the principle of focalization, they can frame a distant view or a specific feature such as a fountain, sundial or pond. Arches lend a feeling of intimacy and enclosure as you pass under them, creating a shift of mood along a passage. Moving underneath an arch typically marks a very agreeable transition from one area of a garden into another; few people are immune to their charms.

The standard size for an arch used at a nodal point is 7'–6" top to bottom by 5' in width. This is one garden feature that can successfully be purchased "off the rack." In rustic settings, arches are often custom built. For example, in North Carolina a vernacular style is a flat-topped arbor constructed with honey locust twigs and branches still encrusted with the silvery green lichen.

Many plant materials can be trained to gracefully drape over arches. Some favorites, depending on climatic zone, include Carolina Jessamine (*Gelsemium sempervirens*), Old Blush Rose (*Clematis armandii*), *Clematis* 'Nellie Moser' and *Lonicera heckrottii*. A rounded 30" boxwood on either side of the arch will ground it.

Pergolas

Pergolas are used almost as frequently as arches, especially where a stronger entry feeling is required, such as between two garden rooms. Pergolas can be positioned at a node or along a linkage. They give a bit more scope than arches for designing a structure that complements the architecture of the house; they can be equipped with benches on either side for a pause. With both pergolas and arches, patterns of light and shade shimmering and flickering on the ground below add a dynamic element that is subtle but highly effective. (Note: People often interchange the terms *pergola* and *arbor*; distinguish them by function—you walk through a pergola but sit under an arbor.)

Gates

Gates are narrowing apertures that funnel you out of one space and into another while signaling a conclusion to one environment and the introduction to another. As such, they stir up all kinds of experiences and are probably one of the most evocative elements you can add to a landscape design.

Gates can be as personalized as a stylish outfit. As purely visual elements, they can be crafted in a variety of specific architectural styles and corresponding materials. They make substantial contributions to helping build or reinforce the genius loci when architectural style and materials reinforce that of the house and surroundings. For example, gates for a town house might be made of wrought iron with classical motifs. For a rural cottage, well-worn, weathered planks set in metal rims would be perfect.

One particularly nice thing about gates is that they inevitably slow you down and get you to interact with your surroundings. They can create highly refined moments such as that private feeling one has while unlatching a gate and being momentarily suspended in time and space.

ABOVE: Since we are often asked to find antique gates, when we spot a pretty one it goes into the "future" category. This fantastic gate was found in Birmingham, Alabama, and ended up in the garden of Nashville interior designer Mark Simmons.

The Anatomy of a Gate

A tip to designing gates is that two gates are often better than one. When an opening is larger than 36" wide, a wooden gate becomes quite heavy and requires a considerable amount of room to open.

If a 36" gate is split into two panels of 18" each or a 5' gate is split into 30" panels, a pleasant proportion results. One side can be stabilized with a cotter pin set into a sleeve at the base, allowing the other to be locked or opened.

TOP: Gates with arches usually require reinforcement along the top. In this 3'-wide x 4'-tall gate, a continuous strap hinge links one side to another. It is painted to match the house.

ABOVE: Really pretty decorative hinges are hard to find. These carry the weight of the wooden gate by bolting 5" securely into the post to prevent sagging.

Steps

A major residential project is rarely finished without a change of the grade, or fall, of the land. Why? For one thing, changes in slope are often required for functional reasons no homeowner would want to overlook, such as to ensure that water drains away from the house properly. In addition, the contour of the land is often sculpted and reshaped for purely aesthetic reasons. This design treatment remains one of the most powerful tools for adding sophistication to a property. Many times, only a change in grade—adding height or taking it away—will give a property the impact it is capable of possessing.

Often, the grade change is intentionally subtle and underplayed. Alternatively, slight changes in grade can be dramatized so they become the feature of the garden that's most unforgettable.

Looking back to outstanding historic examples, it is the Italian gardens in which grade changes are exploited to the maximum. Steep drops and rises in terrain help to create the architecturally dramatic and eventful Italianate garden such as Villa Arcetri, near Florence. A plunging stairway pairs with a high retaining wall. All of these dimensions add a feeling of breathtaking transitions through canyon-like spaces and elevated plateaus.

The French, on the other hand, have historically tended to emphasize flatness and implement grade changes conservatively. Gardens such as Vaux-le-Vicomte or Versailles offer very gradual transitions that orchestrate a slow and stately pace.

On lawns and other open spaces in the landscape, designs tend toward more gradual changes and comfortable transitions rather than dramatic. However, the installation of a very grand staircase can be as a transition from a high terrace down to the garden below. For dramatic effect, add a statue or grotto as part of the structure.

A rule of thumb is not to climb more than three feet without a pause. This is six steps and often the entire journey. If there is more eleva-

TOP: Our take on the British Lutyens circular garden steps is distilled using a combination of Smoky Mountain stone walls and irregular bluestone step treads. Using grass set with stepping-stones, an informal landing is created in the central circle.

ABOVE: At Misarden in Gloucestershire, this set of twelve 6" stone risers set 3' apart creates a grass step system that flows effortlessly up a hill. Over a rise of 10', these steps offer a transition from the flower garden to the main terrace of this stately home. The added bonus occurs at the base of each step, where a 4" planter provides a safe harbor for annual plantings of allysum or lobelia.

tion, install a landing before beginning the next flight of steps.

The style and shape of steps have a major impact on the genius loci of your property. Though complicated and relatively expensive to install, English circular steps are a favorite design treatment for a grade change of about three to four feet. They work well with many types of house architecture, providing that the materials harmonize with the rest of the property. Their round treads add curves and charm to a linear spot.

Another possible treatment is the installation of elegant 18" bands of limestone as a transitional element every 5' to 8', making a slow ascent. These "step ramps" allow you to float gracefully uphill. The rise is approximately

12" over a 5' distance and the width varies from 30" to several feet wide. This device creates ribbons of movement and a strong sense of structure. The pale cream color of limestone contrasts with green grass and vividly animates the ground plane.

Steps may be made from more than one material. The blending of materials creates interest and adds to the feeling that a structure has always been there. Weathered brick and bluestone are an especially handsome combination and look good in a variety of settings. For rural or rustic properties, intensify the feeling of a woodland garden with steps in which the material is the most outstanding feature. The combination of wooden timbers and larger, rougher fieldstones suggests a particularly rustic feel.

All of the passages on a property—the linkages and nodes combined—create an indelible sense of a property's personality. You may not realize it consciously, but passages can have enormous control over your pace—what the ground texture feels like on the soles of your feet and sounds like to your ears, what you are drawn toward and what suddenly surprises you as you make your way around a property. Passages provide the visual power of the ground plane, and the extent to which a property expresses its own unique identity; however, they are only half of this last part of the master plan. Passages largely exist to make it possible to reach desirable garden places.

Step Anatomy

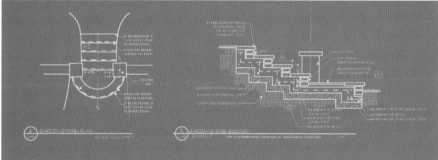

A gradual or sharp ascent (or descent) is achieved through the ratios embedded in the two main elements of steps: the tread and the riser. The riser is the amount of elevation you climb with each step; the tread is the horizontal platform you step onto. When the height of the riser is relatively shallow—such as 4"—the width of the tread needs to be wide—14" to 18". This allows for a slow and secure pacing. If the riser is steeper (e.g., 6") the tread should be narrower (e.g., 12"). In general, the wider the tread, the shorter the riser. Well-designed steps can provide an exclamation, an invitation and even an informal place to sit (or perch).

Creating Timeless Landscapes

When you reach a well-designed garden destination, you have the distinct feeling of being someplace extraordinary. Destinations devoted to the cultivation and display of flowers, herbs and vegetables are one ingredient in the site plan. If not near the house, specialty gardens are specific destinations along a circulation route.

A formal flower garden or place to cut flowers is often part of a master plan. This usually means that a level space is divided into symmetrically arranged, geometrically shaped flower beds. The controlling influence is a pattern of pathways that allows movement around the beds while at the same time giving the garden its embedded structure.

Having said that, it is perfectly possible for a formal garden to be based on a central circular shape with a combination of straight and curved paths surrounding it.

Probably the most defining feature of a formal garden is symmetry. What is placed on one side is mirrored on the other. Shapes are repeated and reflected. Part of the fun of designing formal flower gardens is that within a crisp geometric structure, you can introduce relaxed elements to bring out a comfortable combination of tight structure and loose accents.

Two twentieth-century garden designers who have done as much as anyone to popularize formal gardens as part of a property's repertoire of destinations are the late Rosemary Verey and Sir Roy Strong. Rosemary Verey

RIGHT: This pretty captured view, seen from the master suite, has a formal garden. The center-piece is a foster holly under-planted with germander and Kingsville boxwoods.

BELOW: The Laskett.

FACING: Cone dwarf Hugendorf holly and variegated boxwood edging enliven the kitchen garden at our home. Our paths are 24" wide and planted with mazus and golden creeping jenny between the stepping-stones.

Formal Garden Design

Formal gardens have strong geometric patterns with an emphasis on evergreen hedges. Today, landscape designs featuring formal gardens may occur on any size of property, from courtyard gardens to large estates, and are usually walled or hedged as enclosed rooms.

designed wonderful examples of formal, beautifully planted garden spaces. Sir Roy Strong and Julia, his late wife, composed a variety of ravishing garden rooms that fit the definition—loose as it is—of formal gardens. Their genius was not only in designing the shapes and patterns for the structure of each but also in accenting the nodes with perfectly proportioned urns, pots and other examples of garden ornament; many are very original in execution and spirit.

A formal garden is often a catchall description for a bilaterally symmetrical layout with evergreen or boxwood edging to hold the form. Usually a formal garden contains a circle surrounded by a path and divided into four quarters. It can be planted with flowers or it can be a kitchen garden.

A parterre is somewhat different. A parterre is laid out in a formal pattern that is usually marked out with low evergreen hedges and filled in with annual bedding

plants or gravel. It can also be embroidered (*parterre de broderie*), whereby arabesques of evergreen material are set in a field of contrasting stone. Parterres usually come in twos and are situated at the front or back of a house in alignment with the main path to the door. They are seen most frequently in French chateaux.

Often, the paths in a formal garden are most beautiful when grassed. In most formal gardens, however, the pathways are usually surfaced with brick, stone or a material such as gravel or sand shell. The color and materials selected for the pathways is every bit as important as the plant materials that will go into the beds. Sometimes, paths are even more important to establishing the character of the garden and its relationship to the genius loci of the property as a whole.

As in other linkages, blending materials in the pathways of formal gardens is an option. For example, to add structure and

Herbs—especially rosemary—make nice additions to formal flower gardens. The prostrate form of rosemary looks lovely when it escapes the confines of the bed and spills out like a dust ruffle on the path. It makes a beautiful contrast to clipped evergreen forms edging the bed. Don't be afraid to let some of the plants tumble out of the beds; the sense of permissiveness in an otherwise structured environment adds charm. The same is true if you have stepping-stones as the paving material for paths. Allow tiny plants—such as *Mazus repens*, *Veronica repens*, mother of thyme, oregano, Corsican mint and blue star creeper—to grow between the cracks.

Color varies with the seasons; a well-planned formal garden makes full use of seasonal and perennial color. Seasonal annuals billowing from large pots or urns are especially effective when symmetrically placed at entrance nodes to the garden. This allows you to continually add and change color and plant material and refresh fading flowers with fresher ones. Perennials come into play throughout the summer and are best left in the beds.

Most formal gardens include a focal point in their center. A sundial, small fountain, birdbath or statue all work nicely as traditional accents. Well-crafted and carefully scaled contemporary pieces can also work just as well. The choice of the focal point should reinforce the genius loci; also, it's an excellent opportunity to personalize the space. The scale needs to be correct. When in doubt, try a mock-up of an item that gives a good idea of size. Small gardens look best with centerpieces 24" to 30" in height. Often, a plinth or pedestal will be necessary.

visual interest, you can set stepping-stones into a gravel path. This also makes it easier to walk on in the rain or when wearing high heels.

Generally, paths are edged in a sailor course of brick or stone. That is, the bricks are set vertically with the wide surface making the edging band. In some cases, leftover stone from another part of the site can be used as edging. It simply needs to be cut into regular shapes to form a neat edge.

Path edgings strongly reinforce the design; they act as a curbing to give the beds a contained look. We strongly recommend raising beds in a formal garden at least three or four inches. It is better for the roots of plants and drainage, and it gives a crisper look to the composition.

When selecting plant materials, don't overlook evergreen shrubs. For example, boxwoods play an important role in edging beds when kept low; and when used as topiaries

in the corners, they anchor the beds with geometric shapes such as spheres or pyramids—adding to the sense of structure and thus to the sense of formality.

If you can find it, the John's Island, South Carolina, strain of Kingsville boxwood—*Buxus microphylla* 'Compacta' or *Buxus microphylla japonica* 'Morris Midget'—are superlative choices for edging a formal bed. These boxwoods are "clothed to the ground," which means they do not get "leggy." The leaves are very small and fine textured. When you keep it clipped to about 8" high and 6" wide, it gives an edge of handsome proportions.

Flowering shrubs such as camellias, buddelia and/or evergreen topiaries generally look good situated in the center of beds. A frill of flowers fills the remaining spaces. To achieve a softening effect along the edging and borders, add billows of candytuft and thyme alyssum or *Verbena tenuisecta*.

Kitchen Gardens

Kitchen gardens combine herbs, fruit, flowers and vegetables into one contained or enclosed garden space organized along the principles of formal garden design. Even though they are not edible, it is nice to include low evergreen borders, such as Kingsville boxwood or germander, to add strength and year-round interest to the form.

The earliest shape for a kitchen garden, going back to ancient Roman times, is the four-square plan. This is based on a simple cross-axial design that produces four square planting beds with a central node. Another traditional shape for beds in a kitchen garden is long, narrow rectangles. This shape also lends itself to separating plant varieties from one another, and the narrowness makes cultivating plants a bit easier on one's spine.

Usually, the central node is ornamented with a fountain, well or other appropriate feature. It is especially appropriate to see something that involves water, since the kitchen garden is about nourishment and a balance of natural elements. The splash of a fountain also has a cooling effect on hot summer afternoons.

Consider adding fantasy objects that are also functional, such as large tomato cages that look wonderful on their own. Do not make the kitchen garden look like it's all work and no play.

Since a kitchen garden requires continual care through the growing season, it is important to raise the beds. A seating wall of 18" is a convenient height, or simply raise the bed with a 3" reveal sailor course. The best width is 5', which allows access by rake from both sides while standing on the path. Enclosure of the kitchen garden is as important as the garden! Two gates and a 30" fence create a sense of place. It also provides a defense against rabbits and dogs. Hardware cloth sunk 8" into the ground will repel voles at the perimeter.

There are infinite numbers and varieties of plants to fill your beds. Don't overlook French sorrel (a great soup is made from the leaves) and mustard for winter and summer salad greens. Visit a Chinese grocer and get a packet of seeds for unusual and healthy veggies such as bok choy and Chinese cabbage.

FACING: In Alpharetta, Georgia, a courtyard garden with crushed stone paving offers a kitchen garden setting with a copper basin fountain adjacent to a stone home designed by Bill Harrison of Atlanta.

ABOVE: A kitchen garden in the grand tradition brings joy to the owners of this Macon, Georgia, garden where kale, lettuce and cabbages are winter plantings and the summer brings zinnias and millions of cherry tomatoes.

RIGHT: A circular form of the kitchen garden fits into larger spaces and informal settings such as this farm in Newnan, Georgia.

Kitchen Garden Design

Kitchen gardens are the oldest gardens known to mankind. Best described as a rectilinear pattern with four square compartments, kitchen gardens vary widely in size and shape to meet existing spatial needs. Pathways vary from 18" to 5', with the most serviceable being 3' in width.

Flower Borders

The English perennial border has for generations formed the model of what is pictured when we say *flower border*. These examples are quite deep—as much as 7' to 12'. Typically, they are tiered with tall shrubs and flowers in the back forming a hedge, with a huge variety of flowering plants descending in height to the front of the border. Seasonal color and eye-stopping combinations of textures are the hallmarks.

As lovely as they are, the size of English borders—although magnificent—requires more maintenance than is often feasible on contemporary properties. Narrower borders, of about 3½' to 5½', are a more practical alternative. This is especially true of borders on urban or suburban properties. On large rural estates, they can be somewhat deeper, especially if hedged.

Usually, a linkage runs right alongside a flower border, providing the opportunity to use paving materials and colors that can help reinforce the genius loci and tie into the rest of the site. As with other gardens, raise borders and use an edging material such as sailor brick

The composition of flower and shrub borders constitutes the core of most home landscapes. The interface between a neighboring property and yours is ripe for tiered plantings. A full-throttle approach is to first map existing plant materials; determine which are invasive or useful for ornamental or wildlife value. After culling, determine the predominance of shade and sun and choose plants that fit the existing environment.

Tall evergreen and deciduous trees come first in the plan and are worked around remaining plants by spacing them at least 30' apart. Understory trees like kousa dogwoods and redbuds are then inserted into the canopy, spaced 15' apart on staggered intervals for a loose effect.

Flowing bands of large shrubs, including hydrangeas (my all-time favorite), azaleas, camellias, pieris and other flowering shrubs from

your region are spaced about 5' apart. Merge and mingle them in groups of 5-7-9 so they overlap, all the while thinking about seasonal change. When finished, your border is about 20' wide with future shade overhanging each side. A border of this depth will grow up to screen your neighbor's home in three to five years.

The next tier includes the specialty plants that tempt you on nursery shelves, plus annuals and choice perennials. Make a habit of purchasing at least three or five of each item, depending on their cost and size. Group them together, mixing and merging the clumps to flow seasonally and with good cheer. Taller perennials fall at the rear of this border area, which is usually about 3' to 5' deep. Small annuals and edge scramblers occupy the nearest 12" to the path or lawn. An edging is a very important interface for separate mowing functions from garden areas.

Another tip: Remember to use the 2 x 4 method. Chapter 3 has a form for listing plant materials. And always keep in mind the Matrix.

FACING: Old Blush Roses blend with wisteria to cover this iron arbor in Charleston, South Carolina.

LEFT: Remember that a little white or pale yellow dabbed into a larger field of color such as blue or pink, will release the dominant color and saturate your eye.

RIGHT: This deep border is about 5' wide and allows a tiered effect, with perennials and roses planted on the fence.

Hydrangeas

Hydrangeas are a timeless landscape design mainstay. Whole garden industries in France, America and England are built around the propagation of new hydrangea cultivars. *Hydrangea macrophylla* 'Lady in Red' is a great new introduction, featuring purplish leaves and red remontant, lacecap flowers. Pictured above is *H.* "Blue Billows".

or stone. Edging is especially important if the border does not have a path running next to it; the edging forms a crisp line next to the grass and holds the form of the garden. The combination of edging and paving offers many possibilities to create something individual that complements the spirit of place.

In general, flower borders look best if they have a backdrop. For a rural estate this might be a split-rail fence with the view of pastures or woodlands beyond. In the city it might be a low stone wall, a clipped hedge, treillage or the exterior of a building.

The duty of any self-respecting flower border is to offer vibrant bursts of seasonal color and a combination of rich textures appropriate to the scale and setting of the border. In addition, borders need anchoring with evergreens and shrubs that provide structure. The selection of plant materials for borders takes studying the site and, fre-

quently, some trial and error—which is why planting borders is an art form in itself.

Watering the Garden: Irrigation

As insurance policy for new gardens and older trees, in drought stricken climates an irrigation system is essential. This is important in cutting your daily maintenance chores and helping the trees and plants survive when you are away from home for long periods of time. Choose a system that mixes drip for beds with spray for lawn areas. Installing it early means that you will not have to dig up newly established plants, and you will save money in the long run. Pots can also be automatically watered. By all means, harvest your roof water!

Woodland Garden Design Tips

Shade gardens are tricky places to design. Existing woodlands have many indigenous species waiting to be discovered and propagated. Often damp and dark, woodland gardens need special provisions for drainage and pathways.

Shade trees provide great leaf compost, so harvest it carefully, if at all. Spring ephemerals that bloom early, before the leaves come out on the trees, and complete their life cycle in 90 days love well-rotted leaf litter—the detritus of the woodland that holds millions of beneficial bacteria and mycorrhizae.

Encourage your plants to self-seed and create colonies. Nothing is more beautiful than a bank of well-established native vegetation.

If purchasing plants for your woodland, ensure that they are farmed and not wild-harvested. New woodlands take years to establish, so build your soil carefully to create a deep leaf litter mulch for future generations of healthy native plants.

Always keep in mind the 2 x 4 method of designing with evergreen and deciduous plants for year-round interest and while choosing plants in the four sizes: ground cover, ephemerals, shrubs and trees. These guidelines design cover for birds and other wildlife by creating a tiered effect in the woodland with intermediate perches. As new plants grow, they will stretch for the light and give your young woodland an airy appearance.

TOP LEFT: Our former Atlanta, Georgia, garden is perfect for hostas and ligularias under the shade of the oak. A blending of hosta colors and leaf textures is perpetually interesting of dancing ferns. Just remember that in the winter, this patch of ground will be very bare. It helps to have a low-growing evergreen ground cover to fill the void between seasons.

TOP RIGHT: Nothing says shade garden like the fine-leaved texture

ABOVE: Add natural surprises to your garden in the woods.

FACING: A grand water garden accents the grotto beneath this fine stone staircase in Macon, Georgia.

LEFT: This small fountain is 3' wide, contains a small jet and has brick coping.

Staying a Little Longer

Now we come to areas of the landscape that are designed for active recreation or to provide a space for relaxation well away from the house. These include retreats and hidden garden places, pavilions, swim environments, play and activity areas, and ornamental ponds.

We often think of these spots as mini-moments of glory for the owners of a property. Here is where fantasy meets function: these are places to play and relax. This chapter surveys several possible destinations of this kind but is far from exhaustive.

This final part of the master plan concentrates on passages to destinations. Passages, which include linkages and nodes, are designed for reaching special garden places. Areas devoted to the cultivation and display of flowers, herbs and vegetables, frequently part of the perimeter, can be destinations along a circulation route.

Swim Environments Beyond the Perimeter:
Spas, Lap Lanes, Swimming Pools. The most
important factor in the design of a swimming pool as a
destination is that it reinforces the genius loci as a whole,
rather than counteracting it with what are essentially
stereotypes of what a swimming pool environment
usually looks like.

RIGHT ABOVE: The "purple pond" offers our favorite combination of plant materials designed to jazz up an exceptional rectilinear pond. Striped iris add sparkle and vertical interest to the 18"-deep water body.

FACING: This destination pool has a coping of cobblestones lining the pathway and the great lawn embraces the bluestone terrace. French huile and anduze pots provide vertical interest and color by framing the view to the pavilion from the house. The simple arbor has a metal roof.

FACING BELOW: Stepping-stones around a pool provide planting areas that soften the geometry of the pool edge and absorb moisture.

RIGHT BELOW: A vanishing edge drops into a spa at the bottom of the limestone diamond-and-grass-paved terrace and offers a private retreat in a very elegant setting.

Erase from your mind every other swimming pool you've ever seen. This is an opportunity to create something entirely unique. The goal is to integrate the pool and its entire environment with the materials and color palette already at work on the hub and perimeter, and to follow through the fundamental design themes already established throughout the site.

Pools as destinations work hand in glove with the passages designed to reach them. They can be crafted to be very direct and utilitarian or much more whimsical— perhaps threading you through a flower garden or under a pergola. Imagine what you want the journey to feel like and how long it should take. A functional approach to the pool environment is as carefully orchestrated as the approach to the front door of the house.

Ornamental Ponds and Fountains

Often, ornamental ponds such as still pools for lilies and koi, wall fountains and rills are used in conjunction with formal gardens or in courtyards. They can also be destinations in their own right, especially when furnished with comfortable seating. Fountains come in as many forms as can be imagined—from simple to ornate, rustic to formal. Statuary is often used as the centerpiece of a fountain, just as the lower basin of a fountain often has the appearance of a small pond. The sound of trickling or splashing water is pleasant and helps cover sounds of traffic or other disturbing noises. If there is no natural water

flow for the feature, water lines must be installed or systems designed to use harvested water. Most ponds also need some form of filtration, and, if there is no waterfall, aeration might be required. We find that by covering 70 percent of the surface with water plants, algae is kept at bay.

Play and Activity Areas

When space is available, the creation of pleasure grounds associated with children or adult outdoor activity space can be skillfully blended in with the natural landscape. These include the tennis court, croquet lawn, play equipment and casual multipurpose lawn areas. Using equipment is a short-lived

FACING: This refined, stucco, Regency-style house, with pavilion addition by Atlanta architect Jack Davis is axially aligned with the black-bottomed swimming pool. The pool terrace is clad in bluestone to provide unity in this little gem of a landscape.

ABOVE LEFT: A memorial statue of beautiful white marble brings attention to the center of this garden overlooking Grandfather Mountain in North Carolina. A rill feeds it from a cascade above.

ABOVE RIGHT: A koi pond in Atlanta, Georgia, features limestone coping, four pots by Chilstone and a simple boxwood and grass planting palette.

BELOW RIGHT: A mundane garage wall is enlivened by a "tree of life" fountain and iron trellis in this Charlotte, North Carolina, courtyard.

experience on a property. Place it near the house but out of a major view, and include seating for adults who are happy to look on from the wings.

Pavilions

Like swimming environments, pavilions can comfortably serve as functional parts of the perimeter as well as destinations. We've already seen how one can be installed as covered structure near the house—principally for entertaining. When set at a distance away from the house, a pavilion often serves as a major focal point for a captured view or an eye-catcher for a vista. It can be a lovely place to get out of sun or rain, a setting for a picnic or a place to get away from it all for a few minutes. If you want lights for evening activities,

have the electric lines run during the construction phase. Underground lines would be best.

Pavilions on properties located in city or suburban areas would use less-rustic materials to execute the same design. The pavilion and its plantings should be in tune with the genius loci, and the style and materials should blend with or complement those of the hub.

Retreats and Hidden Garden Places

In Scotland, at Mertoun, the home of the Duke and Duchess of Sutherland, we were shown an ancient yew, perhaps 300 years old. It was propped up with thick canes that held sagging branches. Inside, a space perhaps twenty feet square held four chairs, a table and two benches. A family legend holds that

this was a favorite space for after-lunch cigar smoking for shooting parties. No doubt it was a favorite place for lovers as well.

Friends in Charleston, South Carolina, created a similar place from two tall holly trees. Their son suggested placing a bench within the large, cathedral-shaped space created by the interwoven branches of the hollies. The floor is carpeted with dried green leaves, and one simply uncrosses two large branches to gain entry into this serene sanctuary. This secret garden can be entered and exited only through the secret door of tree limbs. It is crafted from nature and is a very special retreat.

Retreat means many things. We often design retreats into our gardens, and occasionally, entire gardens become hidden places

FACING: In Charleston,
South Carolina, the tall
walls of enclosing court-
yards provide an agree-
able backdrop for the
cooling sound of water.
The 18" brick fountain
basin with bluestone
coping is perfect for seating. The antique butterfly
rose (*Rosa chinensis
mutabilis*) graces the
foreground and provides
ten months of color.

to be visited by a select few. The intent is for owners to nourish their souls in the calm glory of nature. A retreat may be of any size, from a small sheltered bench with its back against a tree and an outward view to a built pavilion adjacent to a swimming pool.

Approaching a retreat can be akin to walking into a mystery novel, where suspense builds as the plot unfolds. The paving looks old and the pathway becomes progressively enclosed and / or overgrown. It is mossy, green and quiet. Time has forgotten this place. A feeling of having lost the key to the gate makes this place happen. More often, retreats are not so romantic, but they are still places for a few moments of rest or contemplation.

From approaching the house and arriving there, through perimeter areas and along pathways, you have reached a destination that is part of a well-thought-out, beautifully designed whole, which enhances your property and brings pleasure to the senses.

Step back now and look at your property with new eyes. Informed by the Four-Part Master Plan, your timeless landscape can be both useful and beautiful, enveloping you in the genius loci of your chosen place, connecting with past and future, providing both serenity and energy for the enjoyment and wholeness of you, your family and your friends. Enjoy!

The Four-Part Master Plan Summary

Empower your property by applying the The Four-Part Master Plan! The Approach and Arrival Sequence, The Hub, The Perimeter and Passages to Destinations offer you tools for creating a coherent property that responds to the architecture, the site and your needs in a seamless way.

In the future, when adding a parking area, an improved front walk, an outward-looking view, expanded terrace, a fountain or a new garden area, The Four-Part Master Plan outlined in this book will instruct and inspire you to find realistic, aesthetic solutions.

RESOURCES

ANIMAL CONTROL

CONTECH ELECTRONICS: INTELLIGENT ANIMAL CONTROL
250.652.0755
www.scatmat.com
The ScareCrow, Squirrel Scatter

BUGBAND
www.bugband.net

BENEFICIAL INSECTS

GARDENS ALIVE
5100 Schenley Pl.
Lawrenceburg, IN 47025
513.354.1483
www.gardensalive.com

BULBS

BRENT AND BECKY'S BULBS
7900 Daffodil Ln.
Gloucester, VA 23061
804.693.3966
www.brentandbeckysbulbs.com

SOUTHERN BULB COMPANY
www.southernbulbcompany.com

COMPOSTERS

COMPOSTUMBLER
30 Wright Ave.
Lititz, PA 17543
info@pbm-group.com

EDUCATIONAL PROGRAMS

AMERICAN CERTIFICATE OF LANDSCAPE DESIGN
PO Box 11730
Atlanta, GA 30355
www.ccald.org

FERTILIZERS, SOIL CONDITIONERS & MYCORRHIZAE

BIO-ORGANICS
www.bio-organics.com
888.332.7676
mycorrhizae

BRADFIELD ORGANICS
www.bradfieldorganics.com

CHAPPY'S POWER ORGANICS
www.rootbooster.com
800.604.0444
mycorrhizae

DRAMM
www.dramm.com
Liquid fish and Kelp

EDEN BIOSCIENCE
www.messenger.info

SUSTANE
800.352.9245
www.sustane.com
natural fertilizers and soil builders

VIGORO
www.vigoro.com

FOUNTAINS

FLORENTINE CRAFTSMEN
46-24 28th St.
Long Island City, NY 11101
718.937.7632
www.florentinecraftsmen.com

HADDONSTONE
Logan Gardens
351 Peachtree Hills Ave., Suite 506
Atlanta, GA 30305
404.231.4808

KENNETH LYNCH & SONS
84 Danbury Rd.
Wilton, CT 06897-0488
203.762.8363

OP INTERNATIONAL
2157 Beachwood Terrace
Los Angeles, CA 90068
323.465.4165
Marcsworld@aol.com

FRENCH AND ITALIAN TERRA-COTTA

POTERIE DE LA MADELEINE
Anduze, France
011.33.466.61.6344

SAVANNAH HARDSCAPES
64 McDowell Cr.
Hardeeville, SC 29927
843.784.6060
Glazed French Pots, classic biot, huile, anduze

TUSCAN IMPORTS
1512 Poinsette Rd.
Florence, SC 29505
843.615.3329

VIUVA LAMEGO
Largo Do Intendente, 25
1100-285 Lisboa, Portugal
011.218.852.408
www.viuvalamego.com

GARDEN CLOTHES

EASY GARDENER
www.easygardener.com

FOXGLOVES
888.322.4450
www.foxglovesgardengloves.com

GARDENERS SUPPLY COMPANY
www.gardeners.com

SLOGGERS GARDENWEAR
www.sloggers.com
tunics, vests, pants for gardeners

WEST COUNTY GARDENER
www.westcountygardener.com

GARDEN STUDY ORGANIZATIONS

THE AMERICAN HORTICULTURAL SOCIETY
7931 E. Boulevard Dr.
Alexandria, VA 22308
800.777.7931
www.ahs.org

THE GARDEN CONSERVANCY
PO Box 219
Cold Spring, NY 10516
www.gardenconservancy.org

THE ROYAL HORTICULTURAL SOCIETY
80 Vincent Square
London, England SW1P 2PE
011.20.7834.4333
info@rhs.org.uk; membership@rhs.org.uk

THE ROYAL OAK FOUNDATION
Americans in Alliance with the National Trust
of England, Wales and Northern Ireland
26 Broadway, Suite 950
New York, NY 10004
800.913.6565
www.royal-oak.org

GARDEN TOOLS

BACKSAVER GRIP MBS, INC.
3511 West Green Tree Rd.
PO Box 090528
Milwaukee, WI 53209-0528
800.752.7874

COBRAHEAD, LLC
W9545 Hwy 18
Cambridge, WI 53523
888.332.7676
www.cobrahead.com
Cobrahead weeder & cultivator

EASTMAN IMPEX
www.eastmanimpex.com

FELCO PRUNER
www.felcostore.com

OXO INTERNATIONAL
www.oxo.com

HARDSCAPE MATERIAL

FIELDSTONE CENTER
990 Green St.
Conyers, GA 30012
Contact: Cheryl Gingery
770.483.6770
www.fieldstonecenter.com
Gray and brown tumbled Crab Orchard cobblestones

NEW MEXICO TRAVERTINE
3700 Camino del Llano
Belen, NM 87002
505.864.6300
www.rmstone.com

OLD CAROLINA BRICK
475 Majolica Rd.
Salisbury, NC 28147
704.636.8850
www.handmadebrick.com

IRRIGATION TOOLS

DRAMM
2000 North 18th St.
PO Box 1960
Manitowoc, WI 54221-1960
www.dramm.com

LEEDS COMPLIANT MATERIALS

BELGARD
www.belgard.biz

GRASSPAVE2
Invisible Structures, Inc.
www.grasspave2.com

ECOGRID
888.837.2376
www.terrafirmasolutions.com

Erosion control grids for drives and grassy areas

LIGHTING

CHARLESTON LANTERN COMPANY
112 Meeting St.
Charleston, SC 29401
877.427.5483 or 843.723.2870
www.charlestongaslight.com

KICHLER LIGHTING
7711 E. Pleasant Valley Rd.
PO Box 318010
Cleveland, OH 44131
landscape@kichler.com

NIGHTSCAPING
1705 E. Colton
Redlands, CA 92374
800.544.4840
www.nightscaping.com

VISTA PROFESSIONAL OUTDOOR LIGHTING
1625 Surveyor Ave.
Simi Valley, CA 93063
805.527.0987
www.vistapro.com

OUTDOOR FABRIC

GIATI DESIGNS, INC.
614 Santa Barbara St.
Santa Barbara, CA 93101
805.965.6535

PETER FASANO
964 South Main St.
Great Barrington, MA 01230
413.528.6872

SUNBRELLA
www.sunbrella.com

OUTDOOR FURNITURE

FLORENTINE CRAFTSMEN
46-24 28th St.
Long Island City, NY 11101
Contact: Skip Brown
718.937.7632

MCKINNON & HARRIS
Logan Gardens
351 Peachtree Hills Ave., Suite 506
Atlanta, GA 30305
404.231.4808

WALPOLE WOODWORKERS
Great Falls Center
9867 Georgetown Pike
Great Falls, VA 22066
888.880.4411
www.walpolewoodworkers.com

OUTDOOR WOOD FURNITURE

CHICHESTER
Logan Gardens (at ADAC)
351 Peachtree Hills Ave., Suite 506
Atlanta, GA 30305
404.231.4808

COUNTRY CASUAL
9085 Comprint Ct.
Gaithersburg, MD 20877
Contact: Pat Hermans or Kathy
800.284.8325

FLORENTINE CRAFTSMEN
46-24 28th St.
Long Island City, NY 11101
800.876.3567

JULIAN CHICHESTER (REP: USA HARRY HALL)
33 Parsons Green Ln., Unit 12
London, UK SW6 4HH
011.44.71.371.9055

MUNDER-SKILES, INC.
799 Madison Ave., Floor 3
New York, NY 10021
Contact: Steve Brennan or John Danzer
212.717.0150

WEATHEREND ESTATE FURNITURE
6 Gordon Dr.
Rockland, ME 04841
800.456.6483
Fax 207.594.4968
sales@weatherend.com

PERENNIALS, SHRUBS & ANNUALS

BECKET'S NURSERY WHOLESALE
John's Island, SC 29455
404.633.6598
*Kingsville boxwood—also Steve Miller Classic
Landscape*

FOREST FARM
990 Tetherow Rd.
Williams, OR 97544
541.846.7269
Fax 541.846.6963

GROWERS
www.harrisseeds.com
Plugs of plants for professional growers

GOODNESS GROWS
PO Box 311
Lexington, GA 30648-0311
706.743.5055

HERONSWOOD NURSERY
7530 NE 288th St.
Kingston, WA 98346
360.297.4172

MONROVIA
www.monrovia.com

NOVALIS
www.novalis.com

**PDSI GARDENER'S CONFIDENCE
COLLECTION**
17325 Country Road 68
Loxley, AL 36551
888.922.7374
www.plantdevelopment.com

PROVEN WINNERS COLOR CHOICE
available at local garden centers

SAUL NURSERY
1115 West Nancy Creek Dr. NE
Atlanta, GA 30319
404.257.3339
www.saulnurseries.com

POTS/URNS/STATUARY

CHILSTONE
Victoria Park
Fordcombe Road-Langton Green
Kent, England TN3 ORE
011.44.1892.740866

CROWTHER AT ANTHEMION, LTD.
PO Box 6, Teddington,
Middlesex, England TW11OAS
Contact: Sharon Powell
011.0208.943.4000
www.ornamentalantiques.com

FLORENTINE CRAFTSMEN
46-24 28th St.
Long Island City, NY 11101
Contact: Skip Brown
718.937.7632

HADDONSTONE
Logan Gardens
351 Peachtree Hills Ave., Suite 506
Atlanta, GA 30305
404.231.4808

KENNETH LYNCH & SONS
84 Danbury Rd.
Wilton, CT 06897-0488
203.762.8363

PAPERCRETE
bbmackey@prodigy.net

PLANT LABELS
www.nothyme.com/plantmarkers.cfm

KS PLANT MARKERS
2620 Lake Shore Ave.
Little Canada, MN 55117
651.483.4655

PROFESSIONAL ORGANIZATIONS

**AMERICAN SOCIETY OF LANDSCAPE
ARCHITECTS (ASLA)**
636 Eye St., NW
Washington, DC 20001
888.999.2752
www.asla.org

**ASSOCIATION OF PROFESSIONAL
LANDSCAPE DESIGNERS (APLD)**
717.238.9780
www.apld.org; info@apld.org

TREILLAGE/ARBORS/FENCING

BRATTLEWORKS, INC.
30 Mooney St.
Cambridge, MA 02138
617.864.2110
Fax 617.354.4246
bw@brattleworks.com

COUNTRY CASUAL
9085 Comprint Ct.
Gaithersburg, MD 20877
Contact: Pat Hermans or Kathy
800.284.8325

OLE CHARLESTON FORGE
PO Box 21317
Charleston, SC 29413
www.charlestonblacksmith.com
Contact: Rick Avrett
843.723.3816
Arbors, gates, railings, fence

TROPITONE
Lloyd & Company, Ltd.
4661 Windsor Dr.
Flowery Branch, GA 30542
Contact: Jeff Howe
770.531.9500
lloydco@bellsouth.net

WALPOLE WOODWORKERS
Great Falls Center
9867 Georgetown Pike
Great Falls, VA 22066
888.880.4411
www.walpolewoodworkers.com

WILDFLOWER SETS

BELTON INDUSTRIES, INC.
8613 Roswell Rd.
Atlanta, GA 30350
800.225.4099
antiwash/geojute

ERNST CONVERSATION SEEDS
www.ernstseed.com

GLOSSARY
The Lexicon of the Land

approach and arrival sequence. The approach and arrival sequence takes you from the street to the front door and creates a presence for the house (hub).

arbor. A shaded place formed by plants that are trained to grow around a trellis or other support.

architectural composure. Mass and style of a house.

arrival court. Area in front of the house for dropping off passengers.

asymmetry. An arrangement of dissimilar objects with similar visual weight on each side of an axis.

axis. Straight line that usually ends at a visual element. Lines intersecting at right angles produce cross-axial design.

balustrade. A decorative railing with supporting balusters.

captured view. Scene created from a window or door with a focal point to gardens or eye catchers; special considerations include use of retaining walls to balance a slope or provision of a backdrop.

Chinese scholar's garden. The evocation of the ideal landscape of the spirit, as envisioned in China. Features re-create the five elements of healing (wood, fire, earth, metal and water) and the yin-yang relationship of the Taoist beliefs.

color. Flower and plant choices in the garden, as well as painted ornaments or structures.

courtyard. An outside area surrounded by walls, one or more of them walls of the house.

design documents. Sheets (drawings) made by a design firm and given to the general landscape contractor; they include all drawings necessary for construction.

drive apron. Interface between public road and private drive.

drive corridor. Driveway between the portal and the parking court; special attention given to create a progression, modulating space with plants, banding on the drive, curves and light and shadow.

drive portal. The apron, drive surface, gates, mail box, call assist, lighting, special plants, curb and gutter and edging of a property.

entry node. Part of the approach and arrival sequence; consists of the front door, pots, steps to house and front landing.

focalization. Technique for making order out of chaos by providing a focal point.

form. Shapes, including shapes of plants and lawns.

formal garden. A garden in which straight lines predominate.

front walk. Linkage from the parking court to the front door; special attention given to the material choice to harmonize with the house.

genius loci. Spirit of place; unforgettable atmosphere; special considerations; the diagnostic for site planning.

grading. Earth leveled or built up to establish the proper elevations for proposed construction.

hardscape. Built structures in a garden.

Herme, Herma. Square stone column topped by a bust, usually of Hermes.

historic site. Site that has importance in history and has been preserved.

hub. The property's natural center. The hub is composed of the house, seamlessly integrated into its natural setting and context.

kitchen garden. A garden, preferably near the kitchen, in which vegetable, herbs and flowers are grown.

landing. Area adjacent to the front door or the bottom of a step sequence; a breathing space. Often includes pot ears.

line. Curved or straight edges in the landscape; may be built or implied.

linkage (as it relates to gardens). Walks or paths that link one area or feature to another.

linkage. Route that conveys movement on a property; a pathway between two points. Attention is paid to surface material, edging, width and alignment.

linked perimeter. Several garden rooms closely held to the house.

loggia. A covered, open-sided walkway, often with arches, along one side of a building.

masonry. Stone or brick parts of a structure.

master plan. Plan for the whole property, including the following four parts: approach and arrival sequence, hub, perimeter and passages to destinations.

multipurpose perimeter. Large plateau or earthen terrace, often formed by a retaining wall or fill that creates space close to the house for a multitude of uses; sometimes includes a swimming pool. Special considerations are many, since these perimeters are often on smaller lots or lots with building constraints such as an ocean or stream.

node (garden variety). A stopping place along the way; thought should be given to the landscape features placed at this spot.

node. Place along a path or walkway designed to make you stop, change direction or transition to a new activity.

node. Where a decision is made; place to pause/change direction; special attention given to organizing pathway alignment, seating area, pots, banding, size and surfacing.

parking court. Area designed to park cars; special attention made for function coupled with beauty by careful design of parking spaces, shade trees, drainage, pattern enhancement with parking banding and medallions.

parterre. An ornamental garden laid out in a formal pattern, usually marked out with low evergreen hedges and filled with annual bedding plants.

passages to destinations. A network that animates movement around a property and invites the enjoyment of garden places removed from the house.

pavilion. An ornamental building in a garden used for shelter and entertainment.

pergola. A frame structure of columns with a latticework roof frequently covered with climbing plants.

perimeter. Outdoor spaces wrapped tightly around the house, opening from interior rooms and providing convenient and functional areas for dining, recreation, entertaining or simply sitting still.

piazza. A Charleston, South Carolina, term for loggia or porch.

pot ears. A flair in pavement at a node designed to accommodate two pots on either side; special attention made for width of walk, size of pot, banding, edging and surfacing.

proportion. Use of plants, materials or ornaments that are of appropriate size for their planned use.

repetition. Repeating an element at regular or irregular intervals.

retaining wall. A wall used to make a level place or to hold back earth after its shape has been changed.

rhythm. See repetition.

scale. See proportion.

seating wall. A wall about 17" high and wide enough to sit upon.

site analysis. A drawing which shows the problems or advantages of the property; includes the direction of prevailing winds, sunny and shady places, direction of drainage or lack of drainage, as well as any functional problems.

site inventory. List of existing plants and features.

site plan. Similar to a survey; shows all built features, planting areas, drainage basins and suggested focal points; includes a north arrow and a notation of the scale to which the plan was drawn.

softscape. Plants, mulch and other organic features in the garden.

spirit of place. See genius loci.

staking. The use of wooden stakes or flags to indicate dimensions of features to be built.

step. A means of changing from one elevation to another.

survey. A scale drawing of the property showing property lines, right of way, roads, buildings and large trees; made by a professional surveyor.

symmetry. Balancing of the same or very similar areas/objects on each side of an axis.

terme. Old French for term; boundary marked by a square, tapering column of stone carved at the top with a head and shoulders.

terrace. A level outdoor surface that extends out from the house.

texture. The sizes of leaves, bark and stone, as well as to their roughness or smoothness.

treillage. Trellis or latticework.

vernacular. Architecture common to the ordinary buildings or houses of a region.

vista. Views from the house to the grounds or grounds to the house; also known as outward- or inward-looking views.

wish list. List of plants or features to include, if possible, in the master plan.

Photography Credits

All photographs by Mary Palmer Dargan, ASLA unless otherwise noted. Special thanks to Hugh Dargan, her assistant "grip" and "garden stylist" (especially with a broom). She ran the gamut from 35mm to Hasselblad to Canon EOS 5D. All blame for soft images, bad shadows and tilted architecture rests on her shoulders.

Pauletta Atwood provided the lovely photo of Barnsley on page 23.

Alexander L. Wallace shot the Charleston gardens on pages 68, 141, 142, and 148.

J. F. Bryan photograph on page 122.

Emily Followill photograph on pages 72 and 110.

Maia Highsmith of Special Gardens reshot and styled frontispiece and Page 80 gates.

All photographs are of our designs unless historic or international.

With warm thanks to the garden owners and inspirational gardens that appear in this book in sequential order.

Pat and Carl Hartrampf (Atlanta, GA); Lulu and Larry Frye (Atherton, CA); Toby and Wayne Press (Linville, NC); Sissinghurst (The National Trust, Kent, England); Kiara Balish-Barnett; Ann and Bob Huntoon (Charleston, SC); Ms. Ford Ford 2595 Forrest Way (Dargan, Atlanta, GA); Linda and Dick Cravey (Cashiers, NC); Christine Cozzens and Ron Calabrese (Atlanta, GA); Drs. Bill Kee and Frank Lee (Charleston, SC); Stowe (The National Trust, Wiltshire, England); Arcentri (Sisters of Carita at Villa Agape, Firenze, Italy); Drew and Kellie Reifenberger; Mary and Ted Moore (Atlanta, GA); Tarre and Pete Green (Atlanta, GA); Carol and George Overend (Atlanta, GA); Joy and Alan Greenberg (Atlanta, GA); Angie and Nick Zervos (Charleston, SC); Neva and Bill Fickling (Macon, GA); Buscot (The National Trust, Oxfordshire, England); Barnsley (the late Rosemary Verey, Gloucestershire, England); East Ruston Old Vicarage (Alan Gray and Graham Robeson, Norfolk, England); Duval and Rex Fuqua (Newnan, GA); Stourton House Flower Garden (Anthony and Elizabeth Bullivan, Wiltshire, England); The Orchard (private); Susan and Eric Friberg; Temple St. Claire Carr (Mrs. John Thiemeyer, Charleston, SC); Longwood Gardens (PA); Porter and Randy Hutto (Atlanta, GA); Billings and John Cay; Kreis and Sandy Beall (the Abe: Cashiers, NC); The Laskett (Sir Roy Strong and the late Julia Trevelyan Oman, Herefordshire, England); High Hampton Inn and Country Club (Cashiers, NC); Wendy and Tom Dowden (Cashiers, NC and Sea Island, GA); Linda and Mark Smith (Huntsville, AL); La Frontiera Palace (Lisbon, Portugal); Medway Plantation (the late Gertrude Legendre, Goose Creek, SC);

Melbourne Hall (South Derbyshire, England); the late Betty Koester and Louie Koester (Charleston, SC); Giverny (Foundation Claude Monet, Vernon, France); Hidcote (The National Trust, Gloucestershire, England); Boboli Gardens (Pitti Palace, Firenze, Italy); Villa Barbarigo a Valsanzibio (Conte Fabio Pizzoni Ardeman, nr Vicenza, Italy); Chateau Villandry (Château de Villandry, Loire Valley, France); Stourhead (The National Trust, Wiltshire, England); Cheekwood (Cheekwood Museum of Art, Nashville, TN); The Peto Garden (Iford Manor, Wiltshire, England); 59 Church Street (the late Juliette Staats, Gay Huffman and Catherine Forrester); Monticello (Thomas Jefferson Foundation, Monticello, VA); Huspa Plantation (Nick Jones, Huspa, SC); Rousham (C. Cottrell-Dormer, Steeple Aston, Oxfordshire, England); Chinese Scholars Garden (Vancouver, BC); Libby & the late Theodore Guerard (Charleston, SC); Steve and Regina Hennessy (Cashiers, NC); Ann and Edward Erbesfield (Atlanta, GA); Joanne and Bruce Berryhill (Cashiers, NC); Dianne and John Avlon (Charleston, SC); Castle Howard (Hon. Simon Howard, York, Yorkshire, England); the late Laura Hampton and the late Ambrose Hampton (Lake Murray, SC); Kathleen and Rutledge Young (Charleston, SC); Joanie and Stewart Long (Cashiers, NC); Peggy and J. F. Bryan (Cashiers, NC, and Jacksonville, FL); Bette and Edwin Hines (Atlanta, GA); Ann and Jack Craig (Atlanta, GA); Jim Millis; The Honorable John and Shea Kuhn (Charleston, SC); Susan and Hamilton Arnall (Cashiers, NC); Greyrock at Highgate (Finley Merry and Sandra Brown, Highlands, NC); Peggy and the late Phil Walden (Atlanta, GA); Mrs. Thornton (Gayle) Kennedy (Atlanta, GA); Eleanor and Julian McCamy (Atlanta, GA); Gail and Bob O'Leary (Atlanta, GA); Dorothea and Jolly Rechenberg (Atlanta,

GA); Versailles (The Chateau de Versailles, France); Nina and George Inman (Augusta, GA); Ann and David Hicks (Jacksonville, FL); Mr. and Mrs. Jim Balloun (Atlanta, GA); Vickie and Neil Robinson (Charleston, SC); Pauletta and Bob Atwood (Charlotte, NC); Harriett and Charles Shaffer (Atlanta, GA); Mary and John Huntz (Atlanta, GA); Gail and Booker Dalton (Atlanta, GA); Frannie and Bill Graves (Atlanta, GA); Jessica and Grover Maxwell (Atlanta, GA, and Sea Island, GA); Lib and the late Whistle Smith (Florence, SC); Becky and Dan Beaman (Charleston, SC); Ginger and Peter Evans; Stella Nova at 78 Society Street (Dargan, Charleston, SC); Mrs. Roger P. Hanahan (Charleston, SC); Mimi and the late Robert Cathcart (Charleston, SC); Andrea and Darrell Ferguson (Charleston, SC); Marcie and Joe Marzluff (Charleston, SC); Mrs. Thomas (Jacqueline) Stevenson (Charleston, SC); Julia and Don Rooker (Atlanta, GA); Miss Ray and James Coker (Charleston, SC); Johan Prins and Maria Sindian; Sharon and the late Dick Densmore (Charleston, SC); Bev and Hix Green (Atlanta, GA, and Cashiers, NC); Ann and Larry Klamon (Atlanta, GA); Kim and Tom Noonan and Mary Lee and Morgan Pridemore (Atlanta, GA); Lorainne and Bill Miller (Atlanta, GA); Sissy and Mark Simmons (Nashville, TN); Misarden Park Gardens (Misarden nr Stroud, Gloucestershire, England); Blickling (The National Trust, Alysham, Norfolk, England); Nancy and Bill Kellman (Charleston, SC); Robyn and Keith Russell (Atlanta, GA); Caroline and Peter Finnerty (Atlanta, GA); Jane and Hugh McColl (Charlotte, NC); Nancy and Lewis Glenn (Atlanta, GA); Barbara and Rick Turner (Nashville, TN).

Index

Bold numbers indicate pictures.

A

Abe, The, North Carolina, **102–3**
Activity areas, 181–82
American gardens, 52–**53**, 61
Approach and arrival sequence: landscaping of, 17; importance of, 73; axioms of, 75–77; checklist for, 78–79; case study for, 87
Arbors, 140–42
Arcetri Villa, 163–64
Arches, 161
Architects' scales, **42–43**
Architectural composure, 96–97
Architectural style of home, 96–97
Art elements, 20
Ashlar, 124
Askins, Norman, 95, 105, 112
Asymmetry, 32, 36
Atmosphere, 25
Axial relationships: identifying, 29–31; in own design, 35; in structuring views, 106–7; in pathways, 159
Azulejos, 50, 59–60

B

Balance, 36
Banding, 123, 129
Barnsley House, England, **23**, 54, 56
Baroque gardens, **50**
Base plan, 40, 42–43
Bates, Terry, 161
Borders: perennial, 25; flower and shrub, 172–74
Boxwoods, 169
Brick: in paving, 123, 124; in banding, 129
Briggs, Loutrel W., 61, 127
Buscot Park, England, **23, 56**, 58

C

Camponi family, 59
Captured views, 105, 107–11
Cathedral of St. Philip, Georgia, **66**
Charleston, South Carolina, historic gardens in: axial relationship in, **31**; repetition in, **36**; sunken courtyard in, **38, 60**,
145–46; testing scale in, **39, 41**; style of, 61; water garden in, 62; case study of, **68–69**; walled gardens in, 150–51
Chinese Scholar's Garden, British Columbia, **67**
Choate, Jim, 79
Circulation route, 157
Color: as art element, 26; warm vs. cool, 26, 28; using in own design, 34
Columns, 140–41
Compaction, 44
Construction drawings, 43–45
Cothran, James R., 61
Courtyards, 145–49
Crab Orchard stone, 123, **125**
Cross-axial relationships, 30–31, 159
Curbing, 82

D

Davis, Jack, 181
Delineation: symbols for, 42
Design, basic, 17–18
Design documents, 43–44
Design principles, 20
Design process: methodology of, 21; twelve steps of, 40
Destinations: identifying, 155, 158; types of, 177–83
Dining areas, outdoors, 129–30
Dowden garden, **121**
Downing, A. J., 93
Drip line, 44
Drive surfaces, 82–83
Driveway, 78–79, 82–83
Driveway apron, 82
Dumbarton Oaks, Washington, D.C., 61

E

Edging, 169, 174
Engineer's scale, 42–**43**
English gardens, 48, **52**
Entry node, 78–79
Environmental constraints, 40–42, 95–96
Epistle to Lord Burlington, An, 65
Evergreen shrubs, 169

F

Fall of the land, 42

Ferns, 28–29
Field, of paving, 123
Field conditions, 45
Filoli, California, 61
Fireplaces, outdoor, 130–31, 184
Flagstone, 123
Flow, seamless, 75, 77
Flower gardens, 131
Flowering shrubs, 169, 173
Focalization: can determine line, 25; directs viewer's sight, 31; strengthens axial view, 35, 159; of arches, 161; in formal gardens, 169
Form: in Longwood Gardens, 24–25; as art element, 28; in your own design, 34
Fountainebleau, 52
Fountains, 180–81
Four-Part Master Plan, 17–18
Four-square form, 30–31
Framing device, 31
French gardens, **52**, 58–59, 164
Frontiera, Palácio de, Portugal, **36, 60**, 61
Functional outdoor spaces, 42
Furniture: plan for, 44; in perimeter spaces, 130–31, 135

G

Gamberaia Villa, Italy, **58**–59
Garden Club of America, The, 52
Garden Conservancy, 52
Garden matrix, 43–**44**
Gardens: grill, 130; flower, 131; kitchen, 131, 170–71; formal, 167–69; woodland, 175; hidden, 183–84
Gates, 162–63
Genius loci: guides design process, 21, 63; implementing, 52, 66–67; history of, 64–66; checklist for, 66; of Benjamin Philips House, 68–69; pathways intensify, 158
Giardino Giusti, Italy, 59
Grading: plan for, 44; on pathways, 157–58; for steps, 164–65
Green: as backbone color, 26, 34
Greyrock, Highlands, North Carolina, **98–101**

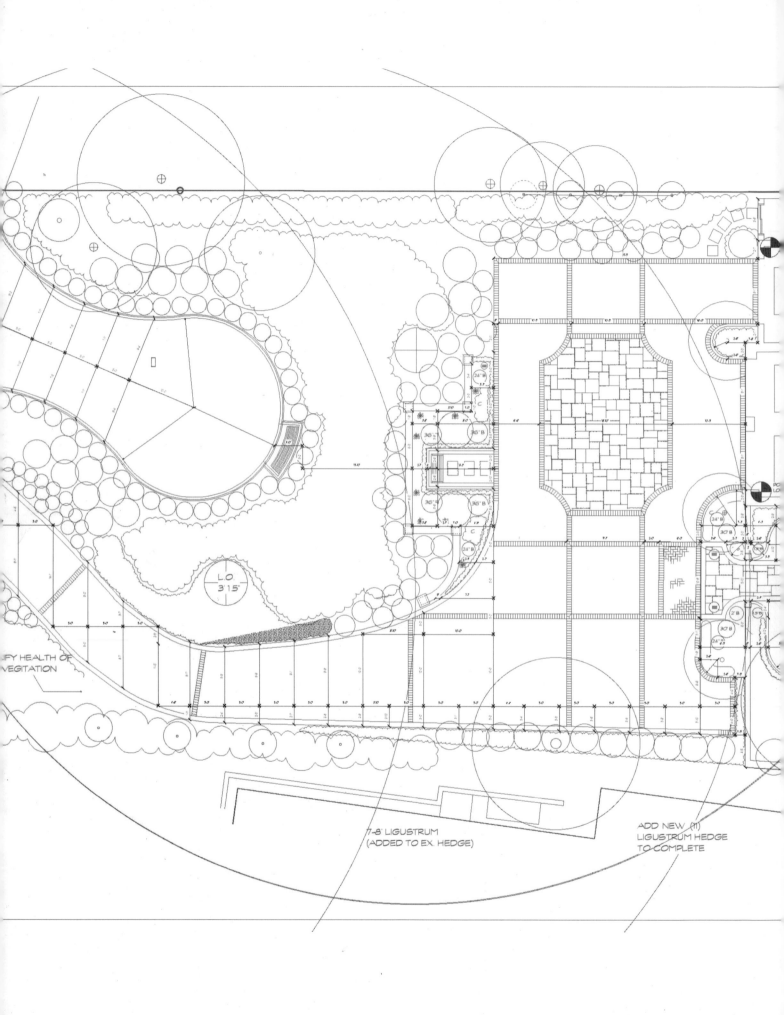

...IFY HEALTH OF
...VEGITATION

7-8' LIGUSTRUM
(ADDED TO EX. HEDGE)

ADD NEW (11)
LIGUSTRUM HEDGE
TO COMPLETE

LO
3'15"